£9.99

Trevor Dennis retired in 2010 after over 16 years on the staff of Chester Cathedral as Canon Chancellor and then Vice Dean. Before that, he was tutor in Old Testament Studies and latterly Vice-Principal at Salisbury and Wells Theological (now Sarum) College, where he wrote his first books for SPCK. *God in our Midst* is his sixth collection of stories and poetic meditations, the first five having been *Speaking of God* (1992), *Imagining God* (1997), *The Three Faces of Christ* (1999, reissued in 2009), *Keeping God Company* (2002) and *God Treads Softly Here* (2004). SPCK has also published four books of his on Old Testament narratives, *Lo and Behold!* (1994, reissued in 2010), *Sarah Laughed* (1994, reissued in 2010), *Looking God in the Eye* (1998) and *Face to Face with God* (1999), and two volumes on narratives in the Gospels, *The Christmas Stories* (2007) and *The Easter Stories* (2008). His children's Bible, *The Book of Books*, was published by Lion Hudson in 2003, and has since been translated into Dutch, German, Welsh and Portuguese. In his retirement he has been speaking at conferences, delivering papers to theological societies or leading retreats in many parts of the UK. He is married to Caroline, and they have four children and three grandchildren.

D1388436

WINCHESTER SCHOOL OF MISSION

06952

GOD IN OUR MIDST

Gospel stories and reflections

Trevor Dennis

First published in Great Britain in 2012

Society for Promoting Christian Knowledge
36 Causton Street
London SW1P 4ST
www.spckpublishing.co.uk

British Library Cataloguing-in-Publication Data
A catalogue record for this book is available from the British Library

ISBN 978–0–281–06927–9
eBook ISBN 978–0–281–06928–6

Typeset by Graphicraft Limited, Hong Kong
First printed in Great Britain by Ashford Colour Press Ltd, Gosport
Subsequently digitally reprinted in Great Britain

eBook by Graphicraft Limited, Hong Kong

Produced on paper from sustainable forests

For Christine,
erstwhile colleague
and dear friend

Contents

Introduction and acknowledgements   ix

1   **Advent, Christmas and Epiphany**   1

Waiting for God   1
What tune are you singing, God?   5
In the dark of the world's turning   9
An old man waiting   14
Anna   19
And we will make our home with them   22

2   **Jesus' ministry**   26

The child in the midst   26
This is the one who came by water and blood   31
'You are my Son, the Beloved; with you
    I am well pleased'   35
The wedding at Cana   40
The calming of the storm   45
'Neither do I condemn you'   51
Transfiguration   56

3   **Holy Week and Easter**   60

He shall not grow old   60
Brother God   65
Pilate   68
They wagged their heads and said   71
Let there be dark!   75
The geode   79
Rebekah's story   80
Joanna   84

Contents

Ruth 89

The breaking of bread 93

Teaching God to dance 97

4 Treasures of the Old Testament 101

Sarah 101

A boy is born 105

Soothing God's face 110

I do not need your grandeur 112

The house of God 115

Views from the mountains 120

5 For special occasions 124

The yew tree 124

This place has fallen silent 127

How must we respond? 132

Words dance in sacred space 135

Remembering Tess 139

The ocean of God's love 143

Introduction and acknowledgements

My eyes were first truly opened to the power of biblical storytelling when I discovered scholarly literary studies of Old Testament narratives. At the time I was teaching Old Testament at Salisbury and Wells Theological College. Some years later I came to the Gospels in what at Salisbury I had mischievously called the Appendix (which most Christians know as the New Testament). I had thought I had known them for years, having been brought up as a Christian and never having left the Church. But I discovered them afresh as four consummate works of art and the Evangelists as artists of creative genius (the Church had *four* of them within its first few decades!). Richard Burridge, in his book *What Are the Gospels?* (Cambridge University Press, 1992), establishes them as ancient biographies, designed not so much to give us all the details of Jesus' life, as to focus upon the question, 'Who was Jesus?' and to answer it by saying that he was and is our Lord and God. The Gospels claim to have a new tale to tell about God, a tale of a God who is born in a peasant family's house and never walks any corridors of power until he is arrested and marked for execution; a tale of a God who consistently puts the last first and the first last, and who overturns not just tables but the rest of the furniture as well; who talks of being a slave and goes beyond talk in kneeling to wash feet; above all, and most mysteriously of all, a God who finally comes out of hiding on a cross, and who then emerges from death still marked with the scars of crucifixion.

How then to release the power of this tale? Well, if the Evangelists were storytellers, masters of the word as well as of the Word, how about storytelling or poetry? It is not the only way, of course, but it is one that I have been following for some years. Again and again I have found composing a story or poem on a biblical passage has allowed me to get deeper into the text than before and to gain a better understanding of what the writer is about. I have relished the room the Gospel stories leave for the imagination, and have taken full advantage of it.

I have always gone to the New Testament scholars first. They have made me notice the detail and its significance (every word counts in the Gospels), helped me to understand the culture that lies behind the material and so catch nuances in the text I would otherwise have missed, and given me new and important questions to explore. Some of them, such as the American writer John Dominic Crossan, I have found truly inspiring (those who know his work will catch echoes of it in the pieces in this book). But the Gospels, for all their originality and bright magnificence, are flawed works. The scholars have helped me appreciate that, too. Each of the Evangelists was trying to come to terms with Jesus of Nazareth, and while each succeeded to a remarkable degree, each of them had their failures – as all Christians have had since, and as we, of course, still do. Two examples will suffice.

First, the Gospels make it clear there were women among Jesus' disciples, and they give names to several of them. They suggest these women were witnesses to Jesus' death and burial, and the first to meet him as the risen, scarred God. All of them put Mary of Magdala in that company, and John in particular presents her as perhaps Jesus' most devoted disciple. If we ask who first told the stories of the crucifixion and resurrection, the Gospels would have us reply, Mary of Magdala and other women disciples. Further to that, and again most significantly, the Gospels suggest that Jesus went against the grain of his society by granting as much honour to women as to men. Yet where in the Gospels are the stories about these women? Neither Mark nor Matthew even mention the women disciples till they get to the cross. Luke devotes two verses to them in chapter 8 of his Gospel, but like the other Evangelists he has no stories of their call. He does include an important story of Jesus with Martha and her sister Mary, and John elaborates further on their great friendship with Jesus: Mary gets to footwashing a chapter before Jesus does, while in the story of the raising of Lazarus, the two sisters occupy centre stage with Jesus, while their brother remains a shadowy figure even after his return to life. John it is who also tells the wonderful story of the meeting between Jesus and an unnamed Samaritan woman, and who gives us the finest example of all in the story of Mary of Magdala finding the risen Jesus. But this is not enough. The Church has hugely exaggerated the imbalance of the Gospels in its subsequent teaching and preaching, its liturgies and its art, but the Evangelists must shoulder some of the blame. In this collection I have tried to give the women of Bethlehem at the birth of Jesus their due, and Anna of Luke 2 also, and have paid careful heed to the role John gives Jesus' mother to play in the story of the wedding at Cana. Four stories in the Holy Week and Easter section I have devoted to women disciples. For two of them I have had to invent names.

The Gospels' casting so much blame onto Jesus' Jewish opponents, and their talking too casually of the responsibility of 'the Jews' for his death, was a mistake of even more catastrophic proportions, though, of course, we cannot lay at their door the hideous anti-Semitism that arose in subsequent generations. The Gospels keep their focus firmly on Jesus and the claims they make for him, and at no point do they make way for another point of view. In the Holy Week and Easter section I have included three pieces from 'the other side', and the second of those addresses the particular charges made in the Gospels against his Jewish detractors.

In its first three sections the book follows the pattern of the Christian year, which, of course, is itself closely based on the plots of the Gospels. Though only two of the Gospels pay any attention to Jesus' birth, all four agree on the significance of his death and resurrection and allow them generous space in their narratives. That is where, so they claim, the truth of it all comes out, and indeed we can say the Gospels demand to be read backwards, since everything that goes before is written in the light of those final events. I would hope it is appropriate, therefore, that the longest section of this book is the one devoted to the Passion, Crucifixion and Resurrection. The final two sections are devoted to pieces that draw their immediate inspiration from the Old Testament, or to pieces written for special occasions. They also were composed in the light of the Gospels, and many of them make explicit use of their material.

This is the sixth collection of my stories and poems that SPCK have published, and I am deeply grateful to their splendid team and most especially to Alison Barr, my editor, whose judgement I trust at every turn, and whose faith in me over the years has been humbling. I could not hope for anyone better to work with.

Almost all the pieces in the collection were composed while I was on the staff of Chester Cathedral. That was a place, like Salisbury and Wells, where I became notorious for my laugh (it is, I am told, unusually loud), which says a great deal about the community there and my former colleagues. They gave me the freedom to be myself and to continue with the habit I had developed at Salisbury of preaching and teaching exactly as I believe, and of mincing as few of my words as possible. When it comes to the Bible we must not pretend; we must tell it straight. The congregation and my fellow clergy at Chester Cathedral allowed me to do that, and I am most grateful to them for it.

I have a few others to thank: our daughter Jo and her husband John for encouraging me to include the piece I wrote for the baptism of their second son, Harry ('You are my Son, the Beloved; with you I am well pleased'); Ann and Stewart for so readily allowing me to include 'Words dance in sacred space', the piece I composed for their wedding service; and my old friends Sally and Malcolm, Pooh and David for granting equally enthusiastic permission for me to put in the funeral address (if it can be called that) 'Remembering Tess'. Andrew Rudd, a Reader and published poet in the Chester Diocese, led a poetry workshop at one of the diocesan clergy conferences, and his enormous skill and encouragement led to my composing the little poem 'The geode'. I read out a first and very clumsy draft of the poem in the workshop, but Andrew had so enthused me, I worked on it again that evening before I went to sleep, and got up early the next morning to do some more.

My wife Caroline is not a Christian and, thank God, has never pretended to be one, but her support and encouragement of my writing have been unfailing. To her, of course, I owe the greatest debt and always will. But friends matter also, especially when they are like Christine Bull, whom I have known for some time now, and who was one of my colleagues at Chester in my final years at the Cathedral. Her preaching is outstanding, as is her faith, her wisdom and pastoral insight and care, and above all her sheer no-nonsense goodness and humanity. To her this book is dedicated with much gratitude and in the full knowledge that it is not nearly enough.

1

Advent, Christmas and Epiphany

Waiting for God

A piece for Advent Sunday. At one point I quote part of Isaiah 64.8: 'Yet, O Lord, you are our Father; we are the clay, and you are our potter; we are all the work of your hand.' Eastgate Street, mentioned in line 5, is one of the main shopping streets in the centre of Chester.

An earlier version of this piece appeared in my book, The Christmas Stories *(SPCK, 2007). The changes made here are very small.*

Once more the wheel of the year has turned.
We are back at the beginning,
at this precious time of waiting.
Four weeks of it.

We have come out of the crush of Eastgate Street
and the queues at the tills,
to this place of waiting,
where we can sit and listen;
a place where the rush stops,
where the television is not switched on
with its nervous chatter of the world's disasters,
and its sorting through the pickings of our wickedness;
no e-mails can reach us here,
and if the mobile phone should ring,
then we will quickly turn it off,

our faces redder than before.
We have turned aside to this patch of holy ground,
to sit and wait,
at this time precisely set aside,
like Lent,
for waiting.
Four weeks now of waiting.
Four weeks!
The insistent world in which we live
would have us want things now,
at the click of a button,
the blink of an eye.
But we have turned aside to wait
in God's good time.

So what are we waiting for?
For God to come and take us home,
to lead us up her garden path,
past trees of Wisdom and of Life,
to open wide the door,
cheer our spirits,
chase off the gloomy clouds of night,
to close the path to misery,
put on the kettle,
sit us down to tea and cake,
and make us laugh again.

As darkness falls we wish to sit with her
and hear her tales,
words that will not pass away.
We want our favourite story once again,
the one we think we know so well,
of journeys and a moving star,
of a birth without pain
and a child who never cries,
of shepherds smelling of angels,

and the wisest of kings bending low with gifts in
    outstretched hands
to a mother who is not tired at all,
and a man who does not mind the child is not his.
We want our make-believe.

God will tell it differently,
if only we will hear.

But that is not for now.
For now we wait, and waiting still, we wait.

Waiting for God is surely a strange occupation,
for God is all about us
in the wild skies,
in clouds unravelled by the wind,
the sun that turns the trees to gold and sea to
    duck-egg blue,
in the gorse that flowers even in the frost,
the shades of winter bracken,
the lifted wings of swans,
the cries of whiffling geese,
in the kindness of strangers,
in acts of unexpected courtesy,
the fresh companionship of old friends,
the love of those whose wedding is near,
the delight of small children,
and the quiet courage of the old;
in the banter of hospital wards,
in all paying of attention and all showing of care,
all understanding and forgiving,
all making of peace,
all whistle-blowing where whistles should be blown,
all standing firm for truth and striving for what
    is just,
all giving and acquiring of dignity,

in all searching and finding of mystery,
and all humility.
We are surrounded by such a cloud of witnesses!
How can we wait for a God who has already arrived?

Because things are not all sweetness and light.
Need I spell it out?
Scratch every arm
and the blood of pain will come fast welling to the
    skin.
We have other tales to tell, if we dare tell them,
even if we are not sitting in the ruins of
    earthquake, flood, fire or riot,
even if we are not holding in exhausted arms our
    precious child,
limp, pain-wracked, dying of hunger,
even if we are not high-walled and road-blocked
    into Bethlehem,
to celebrate the coming of the Christ-child in an
    empty church.
Sometimes it seems God is more than just four
    weeks away.

And so we wait.
We all wait.

What icon shall we carry with us
for this pilgrimage of Advent
(for waiting is not sitting still,
but moving on to God's own destination)?
We are the clay, and you our potter;
We are all the work of your hand.
That will do. Just fine.
We will imagine you,
great God of this vast universe
so far beyond our grasp,

with your hands on the wheel,
holding us together,
keeping us whole,
stopping us flying off at a tangent
to land in pieces on the floor,
pressing us, moulding us,
smoothing us, bending us,
teasing us into shape,
then glazing us, firing us,
holding us up for the light to catch.
This golden image we will take on our journey,
for it brings you so near, O God
(for what could be closer than a potter to her clay?),
and we would dearly love to think of ourselves
as your fine handiwork,
and you dressed in an apron
washing dirty hands and fingernails!
Dressed like that, O God,
you will not seem out of place
when Mary's time has come
and the women gather round.

What tune are you singing, God?

Another Advent piece. The lines I have quoted below sometimes
appear in the readings set for the Eucharist on the Third Sunday
of Advent, just two weeks before Christmas Day.

> *Sing aloud, O daughter Zion;*
> *shout, O Israel!*
> *Rejoice and exult with all your heart,*
> *O daughter Jerusalem!*
>
> *The* LORD, *your God, is in your midst,*
> *a warrior who gives victory;*
> *he will rejoice over you with gladness . . .*

he will exult over you with loud singing
as on a day of festival.

And I will save the lame
and gather the outcast,
and I will change their shame into praise
and renown in all the earth.
At that time I will bring you home.
(Zephaniah 3.14, 17, 18a, 19b-20a)

John said to the crowds that came out to be baptized by him,
'You brood of vipers! Who warned you to flee from the wrath
to come? . . . Even now the axe is lying at the root of the trees;
every tree therefore that does not bear good fruit is cut down
and thrown into the fire . . . I baptize you with water; but
one who is more powerful than I is coming . . . His winnowing-
fork is in his hand, to clear his threshing-floor and to gather
the wheat into his granary; but the chaff he will burn with
unquenchable fire.'   *(Luke 3.7, 9, 16, 17)*

What tune are you singing, God? For pity's sake, after the
violence and threats of the last year, we do not need promises
of yet more from you! Every Christmas the talk is of 'peace
on earth, good will toward men' – and it would be good if the
women and children had their fair share of them too, and the
rest of the earth, which too often we treat with contempt. Every
year we long to hear those words. They flutter with angels'
wings and speak of heaven. They remind us of you.

So what's all this stuff about cutting down trees that don't
bear good fruit and chucking them on the fire? 'The chaff he
will burn with unquenchable fire.' That's what Luke's John the
Baptist promises the Messiah will do when he comes. Well, if
that's what he's coming for this Advent, I'm going to run and
hide. You won't see me here on Christmas Day. I'm not going
to sing jolly carols, or waive my Christmas cheer to greet a
Messiah intent on dancing round a bonfire of the wicked. I've

had a belly-full of Messiahs like that. I want nothing to do with them. There are far too many of them already.

That John the Baptist was quite wrong. The Messiah who fetched up on his river bank declared the leper clean, refused to condemn a woman caught in adultery, honoured the hard man Zacchaeus, put some Galilean fishermen in the same circle as the tax gatherer who'd been taking the best of their catch, caused a scandal by eating with those condemned as sinners, spoke of forgiveness seventy-times-seven, and claimed the precincts of the Temple for those thought not worthy to come near their precious holiness. And where did all this lead? To a dance round a bonfire? To unquenchable fire? No, even the sun's fire was put out for a spell; there was no dancing, only a fighting for breath in the dark.

That vision of you on a cross, God, has stayed with us ever since and will not let us go. It is our icon, written with the gold of heaven. We have carved it, painted it, turned it into song or play. It has put an end to all triumphalism, all dancing round bonfires, all macho gods stoking their unquenchable fires. When you rose from the dead, you lit but a small fire from a few pieces of charcoal, enough for a single fish from the Sea of Galilee and a broken man's remaking. 'Come and have breakfast,' you said. To the friend who'd denied you three times, the one who'd not borne good fruit just when your hunger for it was so sharp, you said, 'Come and have breakfast.' You would have shared it with Judas Iscariot also, had he been there. For him you had to go further than Galilee.

So I'm disconcerted by that warrior god in Zephaniah's poem. That can't be you, God. Have you any idea what this 'daughter Zion' has been through to make that poem? War, invasion, destruction. Zephaniah spells it out in graphic detail. War, invasion, siege, destruction. No, let's get personal. He calls her 'daughter Zion' after all, young woman Zion, young girl Zion perhaps. She's been abused, breached, entered; treated like dirt then trampled into it. By soldiers. She's had her fill of soldiers. So the last thing she wants to hear is the rumble of your tank-tracks as you charge down the road towards her. Nor does she want your revelry. She's had enough of shouting and loud singing and drunken men exulting over her. I know you want to catch her up in your victory dance, but don't you see how terrifying that will be? You'll scare her to death, send her scurrying into a corner, huddled up, hands over her ears, eyes shut, her body rocking, shaking uncontrollably. I know you want to remove her shame, but do it quietly. Take her to the shore of the Sea of Galilee, and invite her to a simple breakfast of fish on a charcoal fire.

Or stick to the end of Zephaniah's poem, to the bit where you 'save the lame and gather the outcast and change their shame into praise', where you hold our hand to take us home. We all want you to come and take us home, God. There are moments for all of us when we don't know where we are any more, when we've gone on our own adventures, or other people's, and got lost. Sometimes there's a nice policeman around, but not always. Sometimes we're on our own, and it's very scary and all we want is to go home. And when we get there, we don't want the house to be empty.

We want your comfort this Advent, God, this Christmas and beyond, not your threats. Threats will not change us, as you would have us change. But your comfort will. That will make us strong, ready to face anything, ready to stand up for what is right and able to do some little good. If you really want to take away our shame and make us whole, if you really want us to find again the dignity you gave us at creation, then hold us, comfort us, take us home, where we belong. Then we'll share our coats and our food with those who have none. Then we'll follow you anywhere, even queue for hours in the hot sun to get through the roadblocks to Bethlehem, or stumble down the narrow, jeering streets to Golgotha, if that is what it takes.

Take us home, God. For a piece of bread and a little wine, or a fish cooked in the garden over a charcoal fire. Or else to show us a child in a manger and bid us kneel.

In the dark of the world's turning

A Christmas piece, first published in my book The Christmas Stories *(I have made a few very small changes to its penultimate lines). It is based on Luke's stories of the birth of Jesus, but not entirely on the version of them generally presented in carol services and nativity plays. Luke mentions no stable, and the word in his Greek text so often translated 'inn' is much better rendered 'guest room'. Those first hearing Luke's stories would have assumed that Joseph's relatives took him and Mary in and gave them shelter (Bethlehem in Luke is where Joseph's family come from), and would have imagined the manger in which the infant Jesus is laid being inside the house – they would have known such a family would have kept their animals under the same roof for the night. There is nothing in Luke to undermine those assumptions, and his story of Jesus' birth in 2.1–7, properly understood against its cultural background, is thus one of warm hospitality. I argue for that reading at greater length in Chapter 12 of* The Christmas Stories.

In the dark of the world's turning
a small light shines.
No flash of an explosion;
none is shaken out of bed,
or terrified out of their wits;
no glare turned into the face,
to make one shield one's eyes
and tremble at the questioning to come;
no beam sent searching the black sky
for enemies, to find them and destroy;
nothing remarkable at all, you might think,
until you see the angels all a-dance.

The good people of Bethlehem and the bad
sleep on undisturbed,
and wake the next day

believing nothing has changed.
Only one family in one small house
has had a sleepless night.
For they could not let a girl
have her child on the street,
or in the cold of a ditch.
They embraced her and her young man
with the warmth of Bethlehem hospitality,
gave her room for the birth,
sent for the neighbours to help.

There was hardly room for them all
in the stumbling dark of the night:
women from the houses next door,
the women of the family,
the grandmother who had seen it all before so
    many times,
the mother who had four of her own,
and the eldest of her daughters,
fetching and carrying,
and standing on tiptoe trying to see,
frightened for this Mary
whom they had never seen before,
who was so young,
so far from home and the women she knew –
no mother to attend her –
so bewildered by it all,
as if she was taken by surprise,
while the waves of pain crashed upon her
and she did not know whether her child
would ever turn towards birth,
or would die shut up inside her,
and she herself would not survive,
but find a shallow grave
so far from Nazareth.

Yet in the dark of the world's turning
the light does shine,
and the narrow streets of Bethlehem
are filled with sheep and goats
led by shepherds
come to warm their hands around the fire of God.
They too have had a sleepless night,
kept awake by angels
who stole their pipes,
brought in drums and trumpets,
turned their quiet fields to carnival,
told them they could not rest
till they had been to Bethlehem and seen for
    themselves.
So they have bent their heads into the house as well,
followed by their animals
to join the ox and ass,
while the women of the family
have brought them food and drink
and they have greeted a young man
they have never seen before,
who says his name is Joseph
and cannot keep the smile off his face.
They stand eating and drinking,
looking into the manger,
seeing for themselves
what the angels said they must see,
knowing they will never be the same again.

And in the dark turning of our world,
that same small light shines
to make us glad
and know we will not be the same again.

Do not mistake,
that child was not born

to drag us screaming into merriment.
We are told by so many at this dark time of
    year
we must be happy,
as if cheerfulness is compulsory,
until the bright festivities are over
and the usual routines are resumed.
Yet that is hard, crushing hard to bear,
if death and grief have come too close;
if the consultant has confirmed too many of
    our fears;
if love has gone cold;
if we are bullied or abused;
if drugs or booze have had their bitter way,
if debt has risen to the roof;
if this Christmas, like the rest, we are alone.

But did you know
one of the shepherds had just lost his wife,
and the mother of the house where the child
    was born
had buried three of her own stillborn,
the last just days before?
They needed more than most to see that child
lying so small, so alive in the hay,
to find the miracle of it all,
to sense the warmth of it coursing through
    their veins,
to know they touched the very Truth of God.

The ground had rocked beneath their feet,
cracked open, leaving them reeling on the edge.
Beside that manger they stood on the world's
    bedrock,
unshakable.
They had not known which way to turn,

but when the child was born they found the gate
    to God's garden.
They had wondered whether anything mattered
    any more,
but then felt God's gentle, strong embrace,
wrapped round to keep them from the cold.

And they knew this child
was not for them alone,
although they held him close.
The truth of this child's birth,
the pain of it,
the fear of it,
the relief of it,
was the world's meaning
and the world's peace.
Nothing else could compare.
They knew that in that house,
no different from the rest,
God himself had come to birth.

And as they gazed upon him lying in the hay,
the old idols came crashing down.
No more the god enthroned in distant splendour,
surrounded by his sycophants;
no more the god who clicked his finger
to decide between life and death;
no more the god who rode into battle,
to leave the ground strewn with the bodies
of those who dared contest his power;
no more the god who shovelled the dead
into the monster's mouth of hell,
lest the comfort of his heaven be disturbed.

The God who had come to birth in Bethlehem
had no power at all,
except the power of love.

And what great power that was, that is!
It fills the hearts of those who look upon him,
it fills the house,
flows down the track towards Jerusalem,
surrounds its grand Temple,
spreads north to Galilee
and far, far beyond,
to reach streets that are strangely quiet
and people here who have been waiting four weeks
    for it to arrive.

So now it is our turn
to offer God our hospitality.

An old man waiting

In the turning of the Christian year, Advent and the Christmas season are followed by the season of Epiphany. That is brought to a close by the Feast of the Presentation of Christ in the Temple, or Candlemas, which draws on the story in Luke 2.21–40. The following poem is a reflection on that beautiful passage, though it treats its details with enormous freedom. It appeared in my book The Christmas Stories.

An old man waiting.
Waiting for his heart's desire,
waiting for his God to move,
to speak those ancient words again,
'Let my people go!'
waiting for him to clear the land of occupation,
waiting for Rome to be put in its place,
waiting for the time
when they will not hurt or destroy
on all his holy mountain,
and the earth will be full of the knowledge of God
as the waters cover the sea.

An old man waiting for justice, for peace,
for the consolation, the contentment of his people,
waiting for the knowledge that all is well,
that no longer will the fetid air sound
to the beat of the helicopter
and the crying beyond all bearing of the mothers
    and their children,
nor the smooth-paved street to the wail of the
    ambulance
rushing to yet more pools of blood
and bodies twitching in the grasp of death.
An old man waiting for his heart's desire,
while the soldiers look down through the smoke
    of sacrifice
upon the courts of the house of God,
to make sure they are kept in good order
and nothing gets out of hand.

An old man waiting.
He has been so for a long time,
waiting for his God to emerge from his hiding
behind that heavy curtain,
to shake off the dust of holiness,
to walk out into the world and see.

He has been waiting all his life for the Messiah,
has this old man Simeon,
like the rest of us,
waiting for a Messiah,
waiting for hope to win the day,
waiting for God to do something,
waiting for a song to sing.

He has been waiting all his life
and this very morning
he opened up his breaking heart
for God to overhear:

'You told me, when my hair was black
and my knees both worked,
that I would not die before your fine Messiah
    came
and hope was born anew.
Well, my God, I wish you to know
that the time now left to me is short –
I can sense it in my bones.
I have been waiting all these years,
through famine, pest and plague,
through settlement and wall of fear
and buses blown to bits,
and here I am, my God,
but not for many weeks or days.
Must I die a hopeless death,
knowing that you do not keep your word?
My eyes are failing fast, my God,
so sooner than I care to say
I will not see him,
if the Messiah comes.
After all this time I will not *see*!
You have disappointed me too long, my
    God.
Do yourself proud before I die!
Let him come, your Messiah,
let him come and bring you from your
    hiding place!
Let me die with hope
knowing it is not all a lie.
Let me sing my song before it is too late,
the music dried up in my throat.'

The curtain bends aside,
enough for a girl from Nazareth
to emerge carrying a child in her arms.

She should have known better, of course.
What was she doing, for God's sake,
in the Holy of Holies?
Feeding him with the milk of her breast?
She slips across the court,
head bent down towards her child,
to leave this Temple and its self-importance
for the hills of Galilee,
for a place where she will not be noticed,
and her child can play.
She is almost out of the Temple now,
when she sees an old man waiting,
and knows full well,
in an instant,
in the twinkling of an eye,
that he is waiting for her,
or rather for her child.
He has waited all his life for this moment,
for her, Mary of Nazareth,
and her small child,
held against the beating of her heart.
How can she refuse him?

So now,
this very moment,
this most holy time,
she stands before him,
waiting for him to notice them.

His eyes are shut against the light;
he cannot look into the sun.
The breeze stirs Mary's skirts,
but he does not catch the movement.
She says nothing,
and he cannot hear the fall of her breath.
And so she adds her waiting to his.

And then the child cries,
and the old man opens his eyes and sees.
'You can sing your song now, old man,'
the young girl says.
'Sing him a lullaby
and calm his fear.
There is too much of it here.'

The old man has not been waiting all this
    time
for such a small Messiah.
But slowly, fighting the pain in his knees,
he stands, straightens, stretches out his arms
to receive the child.
'Oh Mary!'
is all he finds to say.
She smiles at him,
not asking how he knows her name.
Yet still, in his enfolding arms,
the child cries with fear.
'Sing him now your lullaby,'
the young girl says.
'Let him ride home
on the back of your song,
to where we will be safe.
Sing now, old man,
you have been silent for too long.'

So Simeon sings his song,
sings of light and peace,
salvation and glory,
while the young girl turns her skirts
and dances before him,
dark eyes flashing,
bare feet curling, slowly, gently spinning.
To her quiet rhythms

the old man rocks the child,
and all for that time is holy,

and an old woman's fasting days are done.
Anna, exiled Anna,
has come home to Jerusalem,
hoping for her God.
This day,
this hour,
this song,
this dance,
she is not disappointed.
For more years than she can tell,
she has been bent towards the ground,
and never could she sing, even as a girl.
But now, but now
she joins Mary in her rocking dance,
faster, faster,
till they are stamping out their glee
and with the rest of their breath
adding women's voices to the old man's song,
while the child sleeps against his cheek.
Such a day! Such a day!

And still, and still the dance goes on.
Their song is never finished,
nor will ever end its Gloria.

Anna

As the previous piece reminds us, Anna appears in Luke's story of the presentation of Jesus in the Temple (Luke 2.21–40). There she plays second fiddle to Simeon, and we do not hear her speak or sing. Here I have put her centre stage and given her a song to sing to match Simeon's. For the lyrics of her song I have taken my inspiration from Paul's great hymn to love in 1 Corinthians 13.

'One hundred and five, you say. Are you sure?'

'Yes.'

'I thought she was eighty-four.'

'Some of the versions get it wrong. They should have fourteen years before she got married, seven years of marriage, eighty-four after her husband died: one hundred and five in all. It's all multiples of seven: 2×7 + 1×7 + 12×7. Storytelling, you see. Luke had a very tidy mind.'

'But a hundred and five, that's an astonishing age.'

'I'll say. By the time she met Jesus, she was a great-great-great-great-great-grandmother.'

'And you're one of her great-great-great-great-granddaughters.'

'That's right. I was with her in the Temple, when he came.'

'That very day?'

'That very day. At a hundred and five she needed an arm or two to lean on. My mother provided one, and I gave her the other. We used to go home at nights, but every day we were with her in the Temple.'

'So she'd got religion bad.'

'Not at all. She hadn't been in the Temple that long. We came from the tribe of Asher, all of us, including my great-great-great-great-grandfather, Anna's husband. Originally our tribe had had its lands in the hills of western Galilee, but the Assyrians had cleared us out, over seven hundred and fifty years ago. Every single one of us. Took us all to Assyria, except for the ones they killed and those who didn't make the journey. They burned our villages and left our fields for the jackals.

'But we never forgot where we'd come from. The land kept trying to pull us back, and in the end it succeeded. Anna was an old woman when we left. In her 90s. Don't know how she did it, but she did. We went with her. My mother was a widow, too. My father had died when I was three, and my two brothers had both followed him within a year. That was a dark time for us. Anna couldn't see very well at the best of times, and that year was the worst. "Pitch black," she said. Then one day she told my mother, "I'm going home. I want to find some light before I die." That's when we set out for Jerusalem.'

'I thought you came from Galilee.'

'We did, but Anna made straight for Jerusalem and the Temple. We Jews only had one temple, and that's where it was. She wanted to be as close to God as possible, within earshot, you might say.'

'And did she hear him? Did she see him?'

'Oh yes. But not at first. When we arrived, she couldn't hear him above the din of the priests, and she couldn't see him through the smoke of the sacrifices. In any case he was locked away inside the sanctuary and we weren't allowed near. Had to stay in the Court of the Women. God couldn't handle women, apparently, didn't know what to say to them. That's what the men said, anyway, least what they meant.

'But Anna didn't give up. She knew the day would come before she died. She fasted, she prayed, she waited, and in the end she was not disappointed. Though, when God came, right into the Court of the Women, he was rather smaller than she'd expected! I didn't recognize him. His mother was only a couple of years older than me.

'Anna took the baby in her arms, and knew at once she'd come home. She'd found where she belonged; she'd emerged from our fearful darkness. The holy was not to be found in the Holy of Holies. She'd recognized that as soon as we arrived. But she couldn't find it, until it was brought to her in a child just a few weeks old.

'She sang him a song. I can remember some of the words still.

> When I was a child
> I spoke like a child,
> I thought like a child
> turned my mind like a child.
> When I grew to woman,
> I put an end to childish ways,

21

and now this day, this very day,
I can dance in my mind and sing,
'I see you face to face,
my darling God,
I know you fully now,
as I am fully known.
Faith, and hope, and love abide,
these three;
and the greatest of these,
my darling God,
as you know well,
though you are but a tiny child,
so light to hold against my cheek,
the greatest of these is love.'

'A fine song, though I didn't understand it, not till Anna had been dead some years, and my mother too, and I was living in a town in Galilee on the shores of the lake. History had repeated itself too well and my own husband and two sons had died within a year, and I had sunk into the pitch black of depression. Then I met him once again, the child of the Temple now grown to man, grown to teacher and healer. He brought me out of the dark, like Anna all those years before. I became one of his disciples and one of his closest friends.

'Eventually I found myself back in the Temple with him, and he was as disappointed as Anna was when first she came there; went berserk and got himself arrested. But that's another story.

'Then what is your name?'

'Mary. Everyone knows me as Mary of Magdala.'

And we will make our home with them

'Those who love me will keep my word, and my Father will love them, and we will come to them and make our home with them.'
(John 14.23)

'And we will make our home with them.'
What wild talk is this?
If this is human language,
then such reckless presumption is held
in its small compass!
How can we possibly dream such an impossible dream,
of the God of the high universe
choosing to make his home
within the small confinements of our own selves,
within the narrowness of our myopic minds,
the fitful beatings of our hearts,
the dark cupboards of our souls?

Let's face it, God,
you can't come that far down in the world.
It is, after all, of your own making.
Are you so desperate for shelter?
You do not need to come in from the heat of the sun,
or from the cold of the night.
And what do we have to give you?
A cup of tea?
Quite ridiculous.
You could play with our children, I suppose,
yet how could our hospitality be up to the mark?

I have seen you, God,
riding the waves of the great ocean,
or soaring through the heavens.
I have found you in moments of searing beauty,
in the midst of pain and joy,
in the prodigality of generous love.
Only last week I found you in this very place,
in this cathedral church
as I bent in whispered prayer,
holy icons at my back,
over kneeling figures come to find your healing touch,

strength for themselves, or else for those they loved,
traced my thumb over their foreheads
making a sign of a cross,
marking them with holy oil.
You are familiar with the sign of the cross, dear God;
it brings back memories for you,
and the shooting pains of present reality.
So perhaps it's not surprising
that you were there in that case,
though it *was* a surprise, of course,
for always you come as a surprise,
even when you come as quietly and gently as you can,
as you did in the hushed service of healing in the
    Lady Chapel here.
No need for the grand spaces of the Nave,
only for some longing and a few tears,
hands laid on heads,
thumb smudged in consecrated oil.

All right, God,
so your needs are not as extravagant
as we might have imagined.
But come on, God!
Me?
Look, good people are here,
but *us*?
How can any one of us provide you with a home?
Let's face it, we have a hard enough job
creating homes for ourselves and our families,
and we keep on messing things up
for those we love and who love us.
And in our larger families, in our communities,
even such a community as you see before you now, God,
sitting quietly and reasonably attentively in this
    cathedral church,

we have our stresses and our strains,
our huddling for the latest gossip,
our insecurities and hurts,
our little prides,
or our abiding loneliness.
I know there's much more love and holiness
    here than meets the eye,
generosities, heroisms of mind, body and soul
known only to you and the angels.
Yet still, God, it's quite beyond us
to provide you with a fitting home.

Let's put it plainly.
We need plain speaking these days,
and you need it, also, God.
We're simply not big enough.
Nor good enough.
Any of us.
And that's the honest truth.

That being so,
then when you bend your head
to find your lodging here,
when you choose us, as you do,
for your cradling and your comforting,
it can only be for love of us.

And when we find you settled
in the parlour of our souls,
and the air we live and breathe
sings softly with your love,
why then, we might begin
to love ourselves.

Then will we recall you seek no fitting home.
You only seek our company,
to share with us in bread and wine.

2

Jesus' ministry

The child in the midst

In Mark 9.33–37 and parallels in Matthew and Luke we find an extraordinary story of Jesus and a young child. The following piece ranges fairly widely through the Gospels, but has that story at its heart.

The wise men went to the wrong place,
with the wrong expectations
and the wrong gifts.
They went to Jerusalem,
with its high walls, its palaces and shining Temple,
its Herod, High Priest, and clanking soldiers.
They took rare and expensive gifts, fit for a king.
The one they were looking for
was lying helpless
in a peasant's house
in a village a few miles away, off the main roads,
and his mother had never seen gold or
     frankincense or myrrh in her life
and didn't know what to do with them.
They went for a king,
and found God instead.

And we, we follow the same star
and keep going to the wrong place
with the wrong expectations

and boasting in the wrong gifts.
We search for God,
and insist on finding a king instead.

We set God on a high throne,
and surround him with the songs of adoring angels
and our fear.
'He's up in heaven,'
a young girl said,
'and he's on a throne
and it's big, and gold all over,
and he sends people down, down, down to hell.'
We have turned our God into a monster.

And of course, of course, we are so small,
'like grasshoppers', the poet Isaiah said.
And of course, of course, God is quite beyond
    compare,
beyond our imagining, beyond our telling,
beyond a universe whose size we cannot comprehend.
God is the mystery beyond,
quite beyond our grasp . . .

yet not beyond our love,
for we are the apple of her eye,
she hides us in the shadow of her wings,
takes us by the hand,
gathers us in her arms
to bring us home along the desert road,
kneels at our feet to give us water
against the harsh pressing heat,
to place food for the journey in our tired hands.
Within the intimate love of God
there is room for us to soar like eagles,
to spread our wings and turn;
in God's company

we can run and not be weary,
we can walk and not faint.

And now we have a new tale to tell of this most
    ancient God,
one that begins in Bethlehem
and ends on Golgotha
and in a garden to the dead.
A manger becomes the Holy of Holies,
the place where God dwells,
but that cannot hide him;
he must come out into the crowds,
ride a donkey into Jerusalem from the east,
the very day that Pilate enters the city from the
    west, high on his war horse,
with the eagles of the standards shining in the
    Roman sun
(for even the sun belongs to the Emperor),
drums beating, swords drawn.
In wonderful, carefully crafted parody,
Jesus of Nazareth needs borrow a donkey for his
    procession,
to stage God's carnival;
if they insist on calling him 'Messiah',
then let the children proclaim him so,
let an unnamed woman anoint him in a leper's house,
let an ugly, brutal cross be his throne!
And when death cannot hold him in the darkness
    of the tomb,
but must release him into the light of heaven,
then let him still carry the scars of crucifixion
    upon him.

(That is how we recognize God now,
by the holes in his feet and hands,
and the long wound in his side.)

And in between, in the middle of the tale,
he kneels to wash his disciples' feet,
doing the work of a woman slave
or else a prostitute.
No wonder Peter is so outraged!
And in between he takes a child,
a small child, and puts her in the midst,
right in the middle of the circle,
centre stage;
and then he picks her up to cradle in his arms –
when so many children did not live beyond their
    childhood,
when famine, war, disease so often reached them first,
when they had no honour to defend,
but the status of a slave,
the last in the queue,
waiting only to be adults
and then to become the persons they were meant
    to be.
That is how it was in his day.
Let us not be sentimental.

He turns everything back to front,
this man who shows us God.
'If you wish to find God,' he says,
'then look at me holding high this small child.
Do you not see?
Take her in your arms,
And you will find yourself holding me,
bearing the weight of God!
Then you will understand.
Then you will understand what I mean when I say,
"the first must be last and the last first",
and you must be "the slaves of all",
washers of feet.'

(Do not look up to find your God
enthroned above the circle of the earth;
look down to find him at your feet
with towel tied round about his waist.)

If we dare follow Christ where he may lead,
then we will serve,
we can be quite sure of that.

It is hard,
let us not pretend.
We spend our childhoods
vying for our parents' attention
and finding ways of getting it,
or else, if we do not succeed,
we bury our pain to release its force for others' hurt.
And so many shout, as we grow older,
for us to be first,
better, faster, stronger than others;
we have to be good at *something*
or we don't count,
and those who are very good at two things at once,
who can sing *and* dance,
we turn into gods, and lose all sense of proportion.
We compete:
we win, we belong;
we lose, we are pushed out, towards the edge.
We strive to be higher and highest on the league
    tables,
and if we fall, the ground is hard and unforgiving.
We have to impress,
to make our mark,
and blowing our own trumpet is required of us,
for us to be chosen in the first place.
And even the Church is too happily wedded to
    hierarchy.

We too can spend so much precious energy
wondering, arguing, who is the greatest.

Yet if we dare to follow Christ where he may lead,
then we will serve.

Truth to tell, Christian or not, we are all hungry for
     servants,
and when service is given,
generous, open-handed, expecting nothing in
     return,
then we sense at once how very good it is.
We need those who will remind us of the truth,
lead us away from the lures of the Jerusalems of
     this world,
which conceive of greatness in the glamorous terms
     of power,
away to Bethlehem and its women bustling about
an exhausted girl and her child lying in the straw;
who will lead us to that child grown to man,
holding a small girl in his arms,
the child in the midst.

This is the one who came by water and blood

'This is the one who came by water and blood, Jesus Christ, not
with the water only but with the water and the blood' (1 John
5.6a). A piece for the Feast of the Baptism of Christ, composed
when these words from 1 John began the second lesson.

Must we think so soon as this of crucifixion,
of its fearful degradation,
of blood spilled with such unfeeling cruelty?
We have only just taken down the Christmas tree,
and still are singing carols of 'We three kings' and
     'star-led chiefs'.

For God's sake, the magi have not reached
    home yet.
Can we not reserve the blood till Holy Week,
fix our minds for now on the water of Christ's
    baptism
and leave them there?

Yet water and blood,
baptism and crucifixion
are the brackets of this Christ's life,
embracing its meaning,
laying out its truth for us to see and wonder at,
as Sinai Bedouin, running towards us over the
    sharp rock,
lay out their wares on mats upon the desert floor.

All agree, all four Evangelists agree,
that something happened that day
when Jesus came down one evening
to the banks of the Jordan River,
to find John the Baptizer,
felt deep waters fold about him
and then rose up again gasping for the air.

The awaited moment arrived.
He breathed in heaven,
filled the bottom of his lungs with its fragrance,
heard the sound of God walking in the cool of that
    day,
then the voice, as clear as clear,
and knew at once he had found a father.
It was as if his God had run to meet him,
to fling his arms about him,
dress him in his finest robe,
slide the ring of heaven on his finger
(and look it fits exactly!),

bent to put new sandals on his feet,
and sat him down to roast beef
of the most succulent kind,
exactly as the angels like it done,
with all the trimmings of their merriment,
and a piquant sauce of the prophets' recipe.

The sky's ringing dome had covered all humanity,
their psalms and fevered pleading echoed back,
as if not loud enough to penetrate its polished,
   unforgiving surface
to reach the realm of God beyond.
That day a man from the distant hills of Galilee
   heard him speak,
heard him clear as the call of the Laughing Dove,
high in the tree on the river's bank,
'You are my Son,' he said,
'the one I love so,
my delight,
my companion,
spilling over with my energy,
my spirit,
my care!
Run up the road with me,
to meet those who so much need to be embraced,
to be held tight against the world's indifference,
who long to be dressed up and feasted fat on
   fatted calf.
Five loaves and two fish will do as well, you'll
   find;
or else, perhaps, your body and your blood.'

Ah, there it is again,
that dark word of pain,
'blood',
Gospel shorthand for arrest and trial,

for the lash of the whip against the back's stripped
    flesh,
for the dragging of wood through narrow streets,
for the hurling of abuse, the hammering of nails.
Surely we can wait awhile,
this star-bright Epiphany,
before the second bracket is put in place,
to bring the story near its close.

And yet, you see,
God spoke a second time,
at Golgotha.
'This is my son,'
he said,
'my delight,
the one I love so,'
perched like a Mourning Dove on the cross's brutal
    arm.
This man from Galilee,
came with water and blood,
not with the water only
but with the water and the blood.

And so we sing our carols to cold January air,
knowing soon it will be Lent,
time for Allegri's high-soaring 'Miserere',
the gently falling notes of 'Drop, drop, slow tears'.

Yet on this truth we still will take our stand:
the dome of the sky is broken,
the heavens torn apart and left in golden tatters on
    the trampled ground.
To have thought God silent was ever a mistake;
to have imagined him indifferent, an error much
    worse.
God has spoken,

clear as clear,
sung like a nightingale on an English down,
and we have heard his song,
full of grace and truth.
And we have also heard him laugh and say to us,
'You are my son, my daughter,
the one I love,
my delight,
my companion,
and I will dress you in my robe
to honour you,
serve you at my feast,
wash your tired feet;
you will find my spirit, my energy
running like blood through your veins,
you will share my passion, show forth my care,
and then my kingdom will have come on earth,
as it is in heaven,
and my prayer will have been answered.'

This is a time for joy, for joy, for joy.

'You are my Son, the Beloved;
with you I am well pleased'

*The title of this piece is taken from Mark's and Luke's version
of the story of the baptism of Jesus, and I wrote it for the baptism
of our second grandson, Harry. But the Gospel appointed for the
service was the passage in Matthew that immediately follows Jesus'
baptism, his story of the temptation of Jesus in the wilderness.*

So Jesus leaves the crowd at the Jordan,
wet still from the water of his baptism,
with the words of God still ringing in his ears:
'This is my Son, the Beloved,
with whom I am well pleased.'

35

He has seen into heaven,
sensed the free-flying Spirit of God
coming to roost in his own soul,
heard the voice of God,
clear as clear.
He knows where he belongs now.
He is a member of God's family,
his son,
his *son*!
And he knows he gives his father God much
    pleasure,
is precious, cherished, loved.

The Spirit of God
takes him by the hand,
away from that moment
into the wilderness.
Did not Israel leave behind
the waters of their own near-baptism,
and enter into the harshness of the desert?
Did they not spend forty years there?
So Jesus will spend forty days apart,
like them become over-familiar with hunger.

Yet Israel came to the mountain of God,
there found him and all his truth.
Moses went to the top of Mount Sinai
for God to speak to him face to face,
as one speaks to a friend.
Jesus finds the devil, instead.

We too know a world
where the forces of evil and destruction
keep rearing their ugly heads,
a world of too much, too much brutality,
an inner world where greed and fear

too easily take hold.
Goodness seems too small for the job,
and the kingdom of God never seems to come,
except for moments that too quickly pass.
And yet, of course, the forces of darkness
wish us to think and feel precisely that.
'We are invincible!' they cry,
'you will never defeat us!'
They strut their stuff,
tell us all the kingdoms of the world are theirs
and all their splendour.

Jesus of Nazareth does not strut,
but the devil doesn't know that yet.
Jesus of Nazareth, declared the Son of God,
will dress for divinity by tying a towel round
    his waist
to wash the muck of the street from his friends' feet.
The devil hasn't seen him do that yet.
Jesus of Nazareth does not turn stones into bread,
but will take five loaves and two small fish
and with them make a feast so large
that five thousand men
(besides women and children),
with nothing else between them,
except hunger and disease,
will have so much they can't finish it all,
and each man and woman and child
will return home with the words ringing in their
    ears,
'You are my son, my daughter, my beloved,
with you I am well pleased,'
and they will have never heard or seen anything
    like it!
That's what Jesus of Nazareth will do,

and when he comes to the Temple,
he'll arrive at the same time as Pilate,
come as Roman Governor to keep the fragile
	peace,
stretched near breaking point by Passover, that
	Liberation Festival.
Pilate will march in
with clattering hooves of cavalry,
drums beating out his power,
soldiers with their swords held tight in their
	hands,
banners fluttering in the heat of the Jerusalem
	breeze,
hot sun shining from the gold of eagles
held aloft for all to see and tremble at.
The other side of the city
Jesus will ride in on a donkey
surrounded by the peasants of Galilee,
to bring to fulfilment the words of Zechariah,
'Lo, your king comes to you;
triumphant and victorious is he,
humble and riding on a donkey,
on a colt, the foal of a donkey.
He will cut off the chariot from Ephraim
and the warhorse from Jerusalem;
and the battle-bow shall be cut off,
and he shall command peace to the nations;
his dominion shall be from sea to sea.'
Pilate will not be there to greet him,
nor the High Priest.
The children,
the children will cry,
'Hosanna to the Son of David!'
for they will see the truth
and fill the temple with the incense of their glee.

'Ah, yes,' the devil will reply,
'but they will stop him in his tracks,
that Pilate and his High Priest,
and nail the children's Son of David to a cross,
and darkness will fall, most appropriately, over the
    whole land!'

And will you see God in that darkness, Mr Devil?
The curtain of the Temple will be torn from top to
    bottom!
The very Holy of Holies shall be exposed to view,
and just when you think you have him in your
    power,
God will walk free.
Quietly, without any fuss
he will turn the pain,
the desperate loneliness of crucifixion
into the laughter of resurrection.
Will you hear that, Mr Devil?

This world does not belong to you,
whatever you may say.
It belongs to a God marked with nail and spear,
who takes a child as small as Harry Kinley,
or as lively as his brother James,
and says to you,
'My kingdom belongs to such as *these*.
It is a kingdom like no other, do you not see?
And when I take them in my arms
I say to each of them,
"You are my son, my beloved,
with you I am well pleased."

'They have not joined
Pilate's noisy, clanking-proud procession.
They have found another crowd,

with a man riding not a war horse, but a donkey,
and one day,
when they are older,
they may join the children inside the temple courts,
and cry, 'Hosanna to the Son of David!'
They are members of my family,
don't you see?
Sons of mine,
who give me untold pleasure;
precious, cherished,
loved by me beyond knowing.

'Away with you, Satan!
You do not belong here.'

The wedding at Cana

A reflection on the wonderful story in John 2.1–11 of the turning of water into wine, taking careful note of a text where nothing is fortuitous, every detail significant.

A hidden village,
tucked in the hills of Galilee,
guarding its obscurity,
hoping not to be noticed,
Cana, Khirbet Qana el-Jelil,
a name to roll around the tongue
and taste for very sweetness;
'the place of reeds', it means,
where winds make gentle music
and birds weave round nests between tall stems,
an empty ruin, now,
left to the fox and the hyrax,
but once most holy ground,
for the Son of God was known there,
reluctant, put on the back foot by a woman

who could not take no for an answer,
unable in the end to keep his generosity to himself.

There was a wedding, you see,
on the third day,
anticipating resurrection,
a veritable feast,
and God is most at home at feasts –
a feast is what he plans for us all,
when all is well and all manner of things are well,
a feast to declare his lasting commitment and his
    love,
when he will serve
and we will drink the wines from his cellar
laid down for us before the start of time.

There was a wedding,
for a week.
The people of Khirbet Qana el-Jelil cannot quite
    manage a week,
their resources will not stretch to that;
the wine runs out.
The wine runs out!
Such looming disgrace!
Will they ever live it down,
the families of that young man
and the girl beside him,
shyly wondering behind her veil,
splitting the light in all her finery,
as much as they could afford and more?
Will they ever live it down,
that there was not enough,
so the laughter ran out
and the songs became sober
and people no longer danced
but fell to wondering about the evil eye

and how long this particular union would last
before disaster struck,
as so often it did in those dusty streets
so near the sighing of the reeds?
Will they ever live it down?

Yet this is Galilee,
where there are whisperings of God in the air,
the lilies of the field wear the scent of heaven,
and a certain Jesus from the village of Nazareth
    is among the guests.
Anything might happen.
Disgrace might be turned quite all to grace.
You never know;
it has happened before.
This is Galilee, waiting to be God's dancing floor.

Yet would it have happened at all,
if she had not been there, too,
the mother of Jesus,
her name well hidden from our sight,
but not her mind, her determination
that disgrace should once more be turned to grace,
as once it was for her
at the birth of her fine son?
Would he, her son, have moved,
if she had not risen from the circle of the women,
left their ribald songs, turning sour for lack of wine,
and told him to do something?
Would he have sat there,
waiting for his hour to come,
knowing it was not yet,
not till the cross was raised,
the nails driven, and the thorns biting deep?
That would be the time,
the time for God to come out of hiding,

for the curtain to be split,
and all the world to become his holy of holies.
That would be his hour,
not here, in Cana,
out of the way in Galilee,
before he had barely begun.

And so he calls her 'woman',
as a second time he will,
when the cross is his and a circle of thorns all
    his dress.
'Do nothing, woman, it is no concern of ours.'

'Oh yes it is!' says Mary to herself.
'I know nothing, thank God, about a cross.
All I know is this wedding,
and wine run out,
eyes meeting, heads shaking,
two families sinking into shame,
and a young girl and her man
thinking it is all spoiled.'

So, saying nothing to her son,
she turns her head to the servants:
'Do whatever he tells you,' she cries,
in a loud voice that he can also hear,
and then she smiles at him,
triumph in her laughing eyes,
knowing he will have to do *something* now.
Heaven will have to arrive earlier than he had
    planned.
This village wedding turned to water
needs now become the feast of heaven,
and God will have to open his cellar
to bring out the wine laid down before the start
    of time.

He will do it quietly.
He will not do the pouring, as is his wont.
No one will know,
not the bride and groom,
not their families,
nor even the master of the feast,
who has been bearing his own disgrace
that there was only water left.

And so it is, and so it is,
and heaven that day comes to Khirbet Qana el-Jelil,
and all is very well,
and never do they live it down,
and always and for evermore,
till the village is a ruin
and the pilgrims go to the wrong place a few miles
    to the south,
always they will tell of that wedding
when the wine flowed like a living stream,
with such pleasure held in every drop,
such fine generosity,
and the young woman cried for very joy behind
    her veil,
and her young man, also,
and there was much embracing to be done
and dancing wild beneath the stars
and such rare, such precious hope!
And still,
when the last echoes of their laughter
have died upon the Galilee air,
and only the birds call among the reeds,
even then their story will be told,
to make God's merriment.

Mary taught her son a lesson that day:
don't do it by the book.

The calming of the storm

A reflection on Mark's version of the story of Jesus calming the storm on the Sea of Galilee (Mark 4.35–41), with quotations from Job 5.7; Psalms 89.9; 77.16; 104.7; 44.23; 107.28–29; Desmond Tutu, No Future without Forgiveness *(Rider, 1999, p. 76).*

God could have made the world without orchids,
   I suppose,
but God is God, after all,
and there they are,
spotting the dune slacks
with their deep purples, pinks and whites,
and keep eyes sharp for the tiny green pennants
of the common twayblade,
more self-effacing, but as delicate as heaven.
A silver-studded blue,
its name hinting its beauty,
spreads its wings to mark the summer's day,
and a pair dance above the grassy path.
A buzzard turns slowly in the warm, lifting air,
then sits to hunt on its flow.
Across the straits the mountains of Snowdon and
   the Lleyn
soar and fall, soft greys and blues.
The sea is flat calm.

Go back from this year's June
to another October,
a little further south and west,
to a beach they call 'Hell's Mouth',
to a roaring, gale-whipped sea,
waves curling green
to crash and beat the rhythms of the storm.
Balls of spume kicked by the wind from the tops
   of the waves

bowl across the sand,
or fly like small white birds scattering before the
    hawk.
A few children play in their wellington boots
among the spreading skirts of the waves,
yelling their glee as they run and splash and
    scamper their retreats.
This is the sea wild and free,
but for the children and for us, watching from the
    shore,
no danger,
just sheer exhilaration,
lasting refreshment for the soul,
another day to remember
with a joy too deep for pain,
to put in the scrapbook of the memory
among the orchids, the buzzard and the butterflies.

It is not always so.
We do not have to sail single-handed through
    the Himalayas
        of the southern seas
to find ourselves so very small
amid the dangers of the swelling waves.
If we have sailed in nothing more than the *Lady
    Diana*,
sunning ourselves for half an hour up the River
    Dee,
still we can summon from the depths of our
    minds the memory,
even – God help us! – the present reality
of being on board the speck of that boat
caught in the talons of a Galilee storm,
in the dark of a moonless night,
sudden clouds racing over the hills,

gathering unforeseen, unannounced, from all
    sides at once,
hiding the stars,
sky turned black as water,
death, fathoms deep, calling in the howl of
    the wind,
the thin timbers beneath our feet
tossed to one side, to the other,
soon to be overturned, discarded, surely.

Ancient poets, not surprisingly, spoke of gods
    battling the seas,
and in Israel dared to sing of their God piercing
    the sea dragon,
crushing this monster,
cutting it in pieces.
Their words are meant for all those overwhelmed
by the dark forces of chaos
that swell up from the deep,
catch us unawares,
curling over us, waiting to break,
to swamp us quite,
capsize us,
drown us,
pressing us down with the huge weight of the
    abyss.

You know what I mean.
We *are born to trouble,*
as sparks fly upward,
another poet said,
capturing a part of the human condition in
    a handful of words.

Yet we are born, also, you and I,
to trust in God and find peace.

The poets of the Psalms
sang these words also in their prayer to God:
You rule the raging of the sea;
when its waves rise, you still them . . .
When the waters saw you, O God,
when the waters saw you, they writhed in anguish;
the very deep trembled.
Their God could rob the forces of darkness and
      chaos,
steal away their demonic power,
or put a muzzle round their jaws;
he could, as they told it,
rebuke the sea.

Sometimes, in the pitch dark of the storm,
they found such trust in God hard to find.
Then it seemed that God had fallen fast asleep.
Rouse yourself!
Why do you sleep, O Lord?
Awake, do not cast us off for ever!
But then more words of hope:
They cried to the LORD *in their trouble,*
and he brought them out from their distress;
he made the storm be still,
and the waves of the sea were hushed.

'Teacher, is it nothing to you that we are perishing?'
      the disciples say.
They call him 'teacher',
not dreaming they might have the mystery of God
      in the boat.
They do not hear the echoes of those ancient
      prayers,
nor catch the irony of their own words.
It is not the time to savour the niceties of
      language –

there is too much salt on their lips,
too much water threatening to spill down their
   throats
and fill them to the brim.
Yet, and yet they speak to their teacher as if he
   is their God,
as if he has the Creator's ancient mastery over
   the forces of chaos,
power to build a new world, where all is well.
They understand more than they know,
know more than they understand,
sensing his divinity in the corners of their
   souls.
They have more faith
than the story gives them credit for.

Their speech is not misplaced.
He wakes from sleep,
this small figure with them in the boat,
and talks with the wind!
He can speak its language,
'rebuke' it,
like the God of the Psalms.
He talks to the sea, also;
puts it in its place,
as does the God of Genesis and Job.
     'Peace! Be still!' he shouts,
     'Close your mouth!'

Suddenly weary,
the wind collapses and falls,
the sea lies down,
a muzzle fastened on its jaws,
a chain about its neck.
A few words, a few words hurled into the dark,
and all is calm.

Would that it was always so!
Too many a time it is not that simple.
Job, in the story of his suffering,
must wait till chapter 38
before he finds that God is with him.
That poet hits the nail on the head till it hurts,
for so it is, so it can be with us.

And God, what of God?
The Calming of the Storm is not Mark's final word.
His God must go to Gethsemane
to pour out his soul,
go on and on to Golgotha
to spend his body and his blood.
He has the mastery,
yet still it costs him dear.
He has no easy victory.

Nor, too often, do we.
Yet still, still we have God with us in the boat,
even if we only half recognize him,
or think he is asleep and does not care.
And he has, he has, he has the mastery!
A man of our own times,
his faith purified in the furnace of apartheid,
wincing as a small boy at the daily humiliations
    his father had to bear,
bearing them himself as a man of the wrong
    colour,
listening to story after story after story of most
    fearful cruelties,
still can say with all his might
'love is stronger than hate,
life is stronger than death,
light is stronger than darkness,
and laughter, joy, compassion, gentleness and truth

are so much stronger than their ghastly
   counterparts'.
He and Mark join hands,
Desmond Tutu and that ancient storyteller, who
   knew his Psalms so well,
and in the light of resurrection dance the dance
   of truth,
laugh the laughter of heaven.

And we, we have more faith than we know,
more hope than we can understand.
How can that not be so,
when God is with us in the boat?

'Neither do I condemn you'

*The famous story of Jesus' encounter with the woman caught in
adultery is printed in our Bibles in John 7.53—8.11, though
almost everyone agrees it doesn't belong there. It is missing from
many of the early manuscripts of John's Gospel, and its language
and style are much closer to those of Luke. No matter. What
is important is that this story has come down to us, to challenge
and inspire us anew.*

She is left without a name.
She has a husband,
and has committed adultery.
That is all we know.
In truth, we cannot be sure even of that.
We hear the allegations they bring:
'Caught in the very act, she was.'
Are they speaking the truth?
Was she set up?
Was she raped?
Have they made her the perpetrator,
when she was in reality, brutal reality,

the victim?
How old is she?
Is she not long married,
just fifteen, perhaps,
or younger still?

We are left to imagine all sorts of things,
yet one thing is clear:
she is a pawn in clever men's games.
Those who bring her to Jesus have no interest in
    her;
they are using her to trap this teacher who dares
bring the profligate mercy of God into the Temple
    courts
and fling it about like incense,
who tells of an absurd God
running up the road to hold and hold in tight
    embrace,
and kiss as a mother would a returning son;
who says to those hurt and feeling left aside,
'My child, you are always with me,
and all I have is yours.'
'Well, let's see just how far this teacher will go,'
    they say,
'a woman caught in adultery,' they say,
'will you hold *her*, Jesus,
will you smother her with God's kisses,
and tell her all God has, is hers?
It's all very well telling stories, Jesus,
but now let's see whether you practise what you
    preach!
If you don't, then you're a hypocrite, a sham,
and your precious parables are but empty
    words.
But if you do, then everyone will see,

here, here, Jesus, on this most sacred ground,
how offensive your teaching is,
and how impossible your god.'

And so the trap is set.
The woman is caught in the net of their bid for
    power,
in the thin mesh of their desire
to be rid of this pesky preacher from Nazareth.
She flutters her wings no more.
No doubt, she struggled when first she was
    taken,
but now she is quiet,
waiting for the judgement upon her,
waiting for the net to be opened
so she can fly to safety,
or else for the hand to come and twist her neck.
She thinks she knows what the outcome will be.
She waits.

Her accusers wait, also,
while he bends down before her
to draw on the ground
a picture of a mother running up the road
to greet her daughter.
Beside him the girl trembles,
her mind and body snared
in the net her accusers have thrown over her,
while down upon him the questions rain like
    stones;
they want rid of him,
never mind her.

He straightens up.
He does not question her,
but asks her accusers to look within themselves:

'You stand on holy ground,' he says,
'and have you not then found the mercy of God?
Have you not seen her running through the
    smoke of sacrifice
to hold you tight against your fear?
Do you not know God's kisses,
nor feel the warmth of her embrace?
Have you not heard her say, "All I have is yours"?
If you have,
then you will drop the stones from your
    clenched fists,
fold up your net and look this young woman
    in the eye.'

They should then have waited still,
like the woman,
for they would have heard him say,
'Neither do I condemn *you*.'
But, alas, in this small tale,
with so few lines left to run,
they leave too soon,
treading heavily under the weight of
our condemnation.
'Neither do I condemn you,' Jesus says;
but *we* do;
we sit in high judgement upon them,
looking down upon the nakedness of their
    hypocrisy,
exposed so clearly to our gloating eyes.
Jesus has caught them in the act;
we rub our hands with glee,
bend to pick sharp stones to hurl at them
with all the force of our innocence.

The woman, too,
if Jesus won't condemn her,

then we will!
'Look,' we cry, 'the last word of the story
marks her out a sinner.
"From now, no longer sin," Jesus tells her.
So she *has* been a sinner!
She was not the victim, after all,
but seductive, lustful, faithless!'

And that is how we will remember her,

unless, of course, we hear the story's other words
addressed to *us*,
'Let anyone among you who is without sin,
cast the first stone';
and unless we too will wait,
wait with the woman,
to make those other words our own,
'Neither do I condemn you.'

They are most precious words
to keep safe in our pocket for a holy life,
so we can take them out every day
and remind ourselves of what is true.
'Neither do I condemn you.'
They are always on the lips of God,

and what is this life for,
but to travel deeper
into the territory of her forgiveness?
And when we find we are forgiven,
persistently, entirely,
then we will fold up the net
of our own fear-filled hypocrisy,
drop the stones from our fists,
and will be ready,
as ready as we can be,
for resurrection.

Transfiguration

The story of the Transfiguration appears in Mark, Matthew and Luke. This reflection first appeared in my book The Easter Stories – *I have made a very few small changes to that version.*

Finding God at the top of a mountain
is not so very surprising.
Mountains are bigger than we are;
they put things into perspective,
lift us above the humdrum,
remove us from what is routine.
Mountains are never trivial;
they take our breath away.

Peoples have said for millennia
their gods have lived on mountains.
They have talked much sense.
When mountains have not been available
for holy eyes to look upon,
then some have built them for themselves,
great ziggurats puncturing their flat horizons,
to ensure their gods are close,
but not too intimate.
Finding God at the top of a mountain
is not so very surprising.

Had not Moses once met God on Sinai's
    jagged rock?
Had not God called to him
from a cloud bright with divinity?
Had not God talked to him face to face,
as one speaks to a friend,
sharing his secrets with him,
making him his confidant,
causing his face to shine with such a light,

that he dazzled them all
when he walked into the camp,
knowing nothing of it,
until he saw them shielding their eyes,
turning their faces away?
(His face blazed with the light of heaven,
and he did not know it.
How's that for humility?)

And had not Elijah fled to the same mountain,
run home for God's mothering
against the deadly Jezebel?
Had not God spoken with him there,
even though the carnival of wind and quake
    and fire
was that time but an empty show?

Finding God on a mountain
is not so very surprising,
though once, they say,
the devil took Jesus to the top of one,
to show him all the kingdoms of the world,
to make their people seem so very small
and easy for his taking.
But then the devil never did understand
    mountains;
they never took *his* breath away.

What was surprising
was the God we found up there,
for we had heard him many times before,
we knew his tones of voice,
the looks in his eye,
the limp in his gait
(as though he had wrestled with an angel
through long hours of the night).

He was our fellow-traveller,
our master and our slave,
father to us, mother, too,
healer, teacher, brother, friend.
We knew where he came from,
and it was no heavenly city
of jasper, gold and clear as glass,
but Nazareth, a nowhere place.
We knew where he was going:
Jerusalem, to torture and to death.
You cannot have God killed, for God's sake!

Yet there, up there,
on the top of the mountain
we found him,
and recognized him,
for the first time.

He made the strange familiar
and the familiar strange.
His face put the sun in the shade
and his clothes made the wheeling storks look dull.
The rock of the summit,
shaved bare by frost and wind,
was carpeted with flowers,
while far above our heads the eagles gathered for
    the dance.
The mountain leopard lost her shyness,
came out from her hiding,
rolled on her back at his feet
ready to lie down with the kid.
The very air held its breath.

And we?
We did not know what to do with ourselves,
but thought of that ancient tent of meeting,

and supposed one, or three, would be appropriate,
marking a place where heaven touched the earth
and could be found again,
a holy mountain bothy,
built of rams' skins,
pegged firm to hold against the cold and wind.

It was not such a foolish idea,
but this, our new-found God,
was for moving on to another mountain,
the one we call Mount Zion
(too full, as it turned out, of its own importance,
and far too grand a place for the pitching of tents).
Our God would not have us traipsing up our
      mountain,
this mountain of transfiguration,
to bend aside the tent-flaps
and speak with him from time to time.
Our God wanted our companionship on his journey
      to Jerusalem.

And so we gave it to him.
We kept him company,
to Gethsemane, at least,
where we left him to a lonely, abandoned Golgotha.

We had wondered,
when we found him on the mountain,
why his hands and feet were pierced.

3

Holy Week and Easter

------◆◦◆------

He shall not grow old

This piece was composed for a Maundy Thursday Eucharist. Every Eucharist takes us back to that last supper Jesus had with his friends and to the brink of his crucifixion. Each and every Eucharist has a sombre tone to it as a result. But that is especially true of the one held on the evening of Maundy Thursday in Holy Week, when Good Friday is the very next day. Many churches have incorporated the practice of footwashing in their liturgies for that service, and that was the case with the particular Eucharist for which I wrote my poem; indeed, John's story of Jesus washing the feet of his friends was read as the Gospel.

He shall not grow old
as we that are left grow old:
age shall not weary him,
nor the years condemn.
At the going down of the sun
and in the morning
we will remember him.

He died a young and violent death.
Why else should we speak of 'body and *blood*'?
If he had died in his bed,
full of years of sweet contentment,
with Fauré's Requiem,
that 'lullaby of death',

wrapped softly round his head,
we would talk more comfortingly
of 'body and soul'.
But his blood was spilled,
as we all know,
his body broken,
like a young soldier's
on the field of battle.

As the priests in the Temple,
expert butchers that they were,
were cutting the throats
of the Passover lambs
for the pilgrims once more
to cry for freedom,
and eat their meal with God,
so he was nailed tight to wood,
to put him in his place.
With small, unconscious irony
the Roman soldiers put a sponge
on a stalk of hyssop
and offered him vinegar to drink.
Did they know the Passover tale the Jews
    told,
of lamb's blood daubed on lintel and
    doorpost
with a bundle of hyssop?
    Father forgive them,
    for they know not what they do.

There were far greater ironies than that.
To sacrifice,
Latin *sacrificare,*
means to 'make holy'.
And so those same soldiers,
when they nailed him to a cross,

Pilate, when he condemned him
to the most degrading death
in the Roman repertoire,
these together, when they sacrificed him
for the common good,
made him holy,
or truth be told,
set up his holiness on high,
for all the world to see.

Between them Roman soldiers and Jewish
    temple priests
made another Passover,
one needing no vast flocks of lambs,
no Temple reeking with blood,
no lifeless bodies slung over shoulders,
wool still warm against the skin of the neck,
flesh to be roasted, carved and eaten.
At Golgotha,
but a single lamb was slaughtered
for the tale of liberation to be told,
just one lamb for God to invite us all
to his new Passover feast.

Now we have just small discs of bread
and cups of wine as red as blood,
for God to make this meal for us,
invite us to his table,
remind us once again
we are his family,
who need no formality,
no being on stiff, best behaviour,
but call him 'Abba',
a name invented by small children
giving sound to their trust, their intimacy,
and their love.

And see how this 'Abba',
this Father God,
is Mother to us, too,
for she washes our feet,
when we come home,
plays 'this little piggy' with our toes
and makes us wriggle with delight.

Yet on this Maundy Thursday night
the small children are already in their beds.
We are older here,
as were that band of friends
in the upper room,
eating together for the last time,
a last supper
before their Lord's betrayal,
arrest, trial, crucifixion.
Every day since they were small
they had washed their feet,
part of the daily routine,
to be done and no thought given to it.
They had heard of rich people
having women slaves to do the job.
They had heard their friend Joanna speak
of her life in Herod's palace in Tiberias,
where her husband was Steward,
where a woman slave had knelt at her feet
to wash away the dust and the muck.
When Jesus took off his outer robe,
tied a towel around his waist,
poured water into a basin,
washed their feet
and dried them with a towel,
they thought not only of their mothers,
but of that slave woman in Tiberias,

and they were shaken to the core,
glad of Peter's passionate protest.
Still more were they unnerved
when this warm friend of theirs,
their teacher, their healer and their Lord,
said they must do the same,
be mothers or slaves to others:
'you also ought to wash one another's
    feet,' he said,
and they curled up inside
and hid against his words,
as if the world no longer made any sense.

But then nothing made any sense at all
until they met him the other side of death
and all was resurrection.

We cannot talk of that,
not yet.
For this is Maundy Thursday,
with Good Friday but a stone's throw away.
Now we must sit
and let him wash our feet,
and not protest,
and take the disc of bread and sip of wine
for the journey out of our own
    imprisonments,
and when we say
'at the going down of the sun
and in the morning
we will remember him,'
then we must recall his words of reply,
addressed to us as clear as clear,
'you also ought to wash one another's
    feet,
and make my resurrection day!'

Brother God

And so to Pilate's headquarters.

In Monty Python's *Life of Brian*
Pontius Pilate is a buffoon,
a nice buffoon,
played by Michael Palin,
who couldn't play a nasty one if he tried;
he has the crowd rolling on the floor in
    unrestrained hilarity.
The Pilate Jesus faced
was hard as nails,
infamous for his brutality,
all the swagger of Roman might
held in his one person,
with Roman dread of insurrection.

It is the time of Passover,
the worst time of the year
for a Roman Governor of Judea,
when Jerusalem is far too full of people
all come to hear again their ancient tale
of the slaying of sea dragons
and the drowning of soldiers, their chariots and
    their king.
For 'Egypt' read 'Rome',
and you catch at once the stink of Pilate's fear.

It only takes one to start a fire
and the whole city will be ablaze.
Stamp out the flames before they take hold!
If anyone calls himself a king,
or is proclaimed so,
then get him quick,
get him,

thrash him,
to an inch of his life,
then take it,
take the rest
and make his death a spectacle
for others to tremble at;
make it as degrading,
as humiliating, as disgusting as possible.
Let that be Rome's lesson for the day,
so these Jews can still have their Passover,
but know it is but a foolish pretence,
for Rome is stronger than Egypt
and will never be drowned in anyone's Red Sea!

Some began to spit on him,
blindfold his face,
strike him, mock him.
The guards took him then for their beatings.
So we are told.
All that before he reaches Pilate
and the headquarters of Rome.
So now we know what to hold in our mind's eye,
the state he is in:
he stands before Pilate covered in blood,
bruises, spittle.

Pilate looks him up and down:
a wretched little Jew
in his filthy striped pyjamas,
with his swollen face,
teeth already knocked out of him.
He turns, looks out of the window
at the restless crowd below,
and asks his question,
the old question of his power and his fear:
'Are you the king of the Jews?

You, are *you* the king of the Jews?'
He laughs out loud.
It matters not how this upstart Jew,
with his broad peasant face,
his calloused feet and battered flesh,
it matters not how he will answer.
There is only one place
for a man they call 'king of the Jews',
and that is a Roman cross.

He faces him again.
Why does he find it so hard
to look him in the eye and hold his gaze?
He glances at him,
knows in that instant
he can never humiliate him;
the man will always have another cheek to turn,
will never lose his dignity.
He is too close to divinity for comfort,
and that is too dangerous a thought for anyone
    to entertain.
Rome's vast empire has room
for only one divine Caesar at a time;
two is most decidedly a crowd.

Damn him!
Crucify him!
Put a placard on his cross,
tell the world that this,
this apology for a dog, let alone a man,
is 'the king of the Jews'!
Send word to Matthew's magi.
Let them come from the east a second time.
Let them make haste once more to Jerusalem,
this time to Golgotha,
to find what they were looking for

those many years ago,
the one 'born king of the Jews'!
Let them come to Golgotha,
and see!

And if they come all that way,
will they dare to look?

And will we dare to look?
Will we dare to look him in the eye
and hold his gaze?
Dare we see the tears of God?
And will we call him 'king',
or 'brother'?

Pilate

The Gospels do not pretend to give dispassionate portraits of the life of Jesus of Nazareth, and nowhere are their loyalties clearer than in their elaborate stories of his death. They are unashamedly on Jesus' side, and would claim, of course, that he was wholly innocent of any crime. Nevertheless, they are cautious in their portrayal of Pilate. By the time the Gospels were written, the small, scattered Christian communities had already suffered at the hands of Roman authorities, and it was not in their interests to underline the hostility of the Roman governor who had ordered Jesus' crucifixion. Indeed, the Evangelists go out of the way to present him as a reluctant executioner, swayed by an angry mob and the Jewish religious leaders.

This piece is from 'the other side', with all its words put in Pilate's mouth.

How dare you sit in judgement upon me! What would you have done in my position, tell me that?

We'd been keeping an eye on him for a long time. He was very popular. What would he do with such popularity? Some started calling him their Messiah, their new king. We don't need another king. One emperor is enough. Others called him 'Lord', 'Saviour', 'Son of God'. That's high treason. The Emperor bears those titles. Only the Emperor can bear those titles. And he was giving people ideas above their station too, so I heard, not observing proper boundaries. What would they want next? What would he want next?

I was kept fully informed. So I knew full well that he was coming to Jerusalem for the Passover. I heard later about his grand procession through Jericho, and the crowd lining the streets and his asking to lodge for the night in the house of one of our chief tax collectors. I couldn't understand that, when I heard it. Not the way for a Jewish popular leader to retain his precious following, paying such honour to someone like that. The man was clearly a fool. When he got to Jerusalem, his folly was astonishing.

As he was walking up through the dry Judean hills with that motley crowd bleating behind him, I was riding with my soldiers from Caesarea and the lush fields of the coastal plains. This wretched Passover! Caesarea was civilized. Herod had done a proper job when he built it: harbour, amphitheatre, hippodrome, colonnaded streets, aqueduct, a temple to the divine Caesar, fine statues, sea breezes thrown in for good measure, all you need. Jerusalem was a nightmare, with its narrow winding streets, and its religion. Its religion! Far too much of it at the best of times, and Passover was the worst. What were we Romans to make of its Temple? Herod had built that, too, or started it at least. The work was still going on. It was vast, at least its platform. Its gold and shining marble walls would blind you in the midday sun. And in the middle of it a little house for their god. I couldn't fathom its contradictions. It was built to the glory of Herod; that was plain enough. What would the Jews think of it? Would they suppose it was for their glory, too?

The tales they told were dangerous, especially at Passover. All about being under the thumb of Egypt and its Pharaoh, and their God bringing them out into freedom, clearing away the waters of the Red Sea that blocked their path and letting them surge back again over the heads of the Egyptian soldiers pursuing them. 'I will gain glory for myself over Pharaoh and all his army, his chariots and chariot drivers. And the Egyptian shall know that I am the LORD.' The absurd boast of an absurd little god! But the Jews believed it came true. An entire Egyptian army wiped out, and the women with their tambourines leading their ancestors in a wild victory dance on the far shore. That's the story they told every Passover. I didn't need to be a philosopher to work it out. Nor did they.

That's why I rode up from Caesarea to Jerusalem for the Passover every year with enough soldiers to fill the Antonia Fortress to bursting. From there we could look down on the courts of the Jews' Temple and come running straightaway if there was any trouble.

It was a fine procession into the city we had. Drums beating, swords and spears flashing, the eagles of Rome held aloft to catch the rays of the sun. I looked down on it all from my snorting horse. The people in the streets were suitably subdued; the children hid behind their mothers' skirts. No one dared raise so much as a fist to us. They knew well what we would have done if they had. Then one of my centurions brought me a disturbing report. That little peasant from Galilee had mocked me, if not to my face, then right out in the open. He'd borrowed a donkey, saying he would give it back when he'd finished with it, and then he'd ridden into the city from the east, just as I was riding in from the west. This was deliberate mockery, carefully planned, so the centurion told me. 'The people loved it, sir,' he said. I bet they did! Worse was to come. He took the lame and the blind into the Temple, which was against his own religion. A flagrant violation of the rules laid down in his own sacred scrolls. I said the man was a fool. But then he went stark, raving mad. Started overturning everything. Money everywhere, baskets of pigeons broken open and the birds flying free, and the sellers shouting. He stopped the priests and the Levites carrying their precious vessels through the precincts. He was disrupting the entire operation, with Passover almost begun and the Temple and the whole city crammed full of pilgrims. What would you have done? The same as me. Sent in the soldiers at a run and the Jewish Temple police stomping behind them; and when he disappeared, taken any means necessary to find him and arrest him. Then crucifixion. As an example to others.

Caiaphas got it right. 'It is better for you to have one man die for the people, than to have the whole nation destroyed.' Exactly! If I hadn't intervened and killed Jesus, how many others would have died? He would have started a riot, if not a revolution, and if I'd let him carry on, the towns and villages and the whole countryside could have been caught up in it. He could have started a war! I would have lost good men, and you would have had your women raped and your children burned alive or skewered on our spears. Would you have preferred that? I nipped it in the bud. Did what I had to do, what any man in my position would have done. If you think otherwise, then you're as big a fool as he was.

And don't give me those tales about my washing my hands and my wife telling me he was innocent! As for saying I released Barabbas! I am Pontius Pilate, the Roman Governor of Judea, keeping the peace for my Emperor in a particularly troublesome part of his empire. I don't release Barabbases. I get rid of them. Like Jesuses of Nazareth. To keep the peace. To keep people happy. To keep my Emperor happy. And to keep the gods happy, too, if they've got any sense.

If you ever get your own empire, you'll be just the same.

They wagged their heads and said

The Evangelists attempted to play down Pilate's role in the death of Jesus. That was one thing. Their shifting the blame on to Jesus' Jewish contemporaries was quite another, and proved to be utterly disastrous. To be fair to them, they would surely never have written as they did, had they been able to foresee what subsequent generations of Christians would do with their words.

This is a second piece 'from the other side', this time not from the perspective of the Roman authorities, but from that of 'the Jews'.

You have only heard the story from one side. Let me tell it from the other, show you how it was from where we stood. You have demonized us for long enough, called us 'Christ-killers', hauled us off in cattle trucks for poison gas, or slower death by starvation and typhus. It is high time you listened to our story. 'The truth will out on Good Friday,' you say. Quite so. Then hear me out.

'Those who passed by derided him, shaking their heads and saying, "Aha! You who would destroy the temple and build it in three days, save yourself and come down from the cross!"' That is how you tell it, and I know well the psalm you used as your quarry for those sharp-hewn words:

> *All who see me mock at me;*
> *they make mouths at me, they shake their heads;*
> *'Commit your cause to the LORD;*
> *let him deliver –*
> *let him rescue the one in whom he delights!'*

Those bitter words belong to my Scriptures also, yet you have used them most grievously against us. You have turned their mockery upon us. I do not wish to play your games. I will speak calmly, and simply ask you to listen and not interrupt.

You have to understand our precariousness and its history. We have always been at the mercy of others. The story we tell about our people begins with a pharaoh attempting genocide, trying to strangle us at birth, or fling us by our tiny heels into the Nile. And when later we have a land to call our own, too soon we fall under the jackboot of the Assyrians, then the

Babylonians, then the Persians, then the Greeks. Sometimes they try to destroy our religion and our culture. Soon after the Greeks come the Romans, and when we rise in revolt, we discover the might of their legions and the nature of their famous efficiency. Their esteemed Pax Romana means our towns destroyed, villages burned, crops taken or spoiled, our women raped, men slaughtered, children orphaned or killed. And when the killing stops, the threat of still more hangs over us, together with the reality of their taxes.

That is how our story goes, and circumstances such as these teach you to know what is precious and hang on to it with all your strength. You tell the ancient stories over and over, especially the ones that single you out as the beloved people of God, the bearers of his teaching and his promises for the world. And if you cannot take them to the world, because the world will not listen, then you sit in the circle round the fire of your Temple sacrifices and remind each other of your calling and your dignity.

Jesus of Nazareth undid those stories and cast their threads to the winds of Galilee. He told a story of two brothers, full of wonderful echoes of the tales of two brothers in our book of Genesis in the Torah. Only in his version their father treats them both as elder sons. Ridiculous! But much worse than that: if such a father can dress up his younger son in all the trappings of his own authority and present him in public as if he were his elder son, and then still say to the elder brother, 'My child, all that is mine is yours', leaving him with his honour and his position intact, then God can say not just to Isaac and Jacob, but to Ishmael and Esau also, 'My children, all that is mine is yours'. And where does that leave us? Such a story strikes at the heart of our God-given identity. If the parable takes us into the mind of God, as he claimed it did, then we do not know who we are any more. We must go right back to the beginning, to the stories of our ancestors, and tell a new and quite different tale. Impossible.

It was not just what he taught either, but what he did. He forgave people their sins. What use was the Temple then? We only had one Temple in all the world, and it was where forgiveness could be declared and found, secured by sacrifice, kept in good and lively order by priests and Levites. We had a system. He had none, as far as we could see. He put the arms of God round all and sundry, even before they repented. He put forgiveness first, outrageously. What was the Torah for and all the worship of the Temple, if God could pick up his robes and run to meet us, or go looking for us in the desert hills, or rake for us through the dirt on the floor of her house?

That was another thing, you see. The way he spoke of God. Our God is creator of the whole world, so holy we cannot pronounce his name, and he imagined him as an anxious housewife, or worse, acted him out as a woman slave kneeling at our feet, washing off the dirt. Where was the majesty, the glory of God in that? How could we teach our children to fear God and keep the honour of our families? How could we keep our wives in their proper place, for that matter, when he allowed the women who followed him the same dignity as the men? He unravelled our most precious stories and then he yanked the threads of our society. And he claimed the authority to do all this when he was no more than a peasant from Nazareth. He was not an expert in the Torah, nor a priest, and none of us had even heard of Nazareth before he came along. His followers said he took the Holy of Holies around with him, pitched God's ancient tent wherever they stayed for the night. They did not need the Temple, they said, and it only enraged him, they said, because the records of the debts of the poor were kept there, and because, so he believed, it drove widows and their like over the cliff of destitution.

The Temple was magnificent! Don't you see, it was the only magnificence we had! And he wanted to take it all away from us, tear down the curtain from the Holy of Holies, bring God out of his shrine, borrow a donkey for him, and dress him in the clothes of a landless peasant. Too much! Too much! Too much!

We tried hard to make him see sense, but it was no use. We argued with him, as we Jews have always done with one another. Nothing would shift him. He told us God had prepared a party for us in our honour and all we had to do was join the celebrations. As if it were that simple. It was nonsense, dangerous, blasphemous nonsense.

And you, his followers, have come to agree with us, I see. You quickly set upright the tables he overturned. Over the centuries you have put more fear of God into people than we ever did. You have given men back their special honour and found your own Ishmaels and Esaus to drive away from the promises of God. And now you find your backs against the wall, your voices have become shrill, your hearts unforgiving, your minds shut against the light. You, too, have become Christ-killers. What irony! You might have thought at least we would be able to understand each other now.

Let there be dark!

The last of three Good Friday pieces 'from the other side'. I composed it in 2010, at a time when John Venables, who as a boy had joined a friend in murdering little Jamie Bulger, was once more in the news and was provoking great outpourings of anger in both the media and the public at large.

Let there be dark,
oh, let there be dark!
Give me the comforting dark of the bedclothes
pulled up over the head,
burrowing down
to the middle of the bed,
curling tight like a foetus
to listen to my beating heart

as once I heard my mother's
that precious time in her soft womb.
Let me be a small child again,
safe in the warm dark,
hidden from the winging terrors of the night.
Let me be small,
not yet grown tall enough
to face the complexities
of this perplexing world.
Let me cling to childish ignorance,
refusing to unlearn what once I was taught.
Allow me to keep things simple,
straightforward, clear;
like the Bible –
that's simple enough,
its truths lying on the surface,
needing us only to bend down and pick them up,
as comfort blankets to trail behind us,
or stones to hurl at those we choose not to hear or
    understand.

Do not say I don't know best.
I do not wish to entertain uncomfortable truths,
nor be shaken out of my complacency.
Leave me to my cherished beliefs
and let me shut my mind
to cold draughts of knowledge and discovery.
Do not shine your light into the crevices of my mind,
where sharp memories lie and untold hurts.
Let the abuse remain hidden.
'We are all damaged goods,' you say.
Well I would rather not know.
'Know yourself,' is the ancient wisdom.
Count me out.
'Damaged people damage others.'

If I hide under the bedclothes from myself,
then I will not need to ask what I do to others.
I do not wish to see the cracks in my soul,
or have you pick through the garbage of my harm.
The last thing I want is the truth.
I prefer to see what is wrong with *you*.
There. That's honest, isn't it?
Enough to be going on with for now.

This is getting too personal.
I will change the subject,
turn the spotlight on *him*.
'My God, my God, why have you forsaken me?'
That's what he said,
shouted out with all the breath he could muster.
Tell me, was he crying for the father he never knew?
A short history lesson,
then you can answer my question.
He was born in Galilee,
in a hamlet four miles from Sepphoris town,
just before the death of King Herod.
When that cruel Herod died,
the Jews, held down too long,
rose up to claim their dignity,
and brought three legions marching south from
    Syria.
A soldier-man called Gaius captured Sepphoris,
burnt it, herded its people into slavery.
What happened to Nazareth?
We can guess.
Where was Joseph, the carpenter?
Working in Sepphoris?
Did Mary pick up her child and flee?
We know *they* escaped,
but did Joseph not come home,

and did they see the smoke of burning Sepphoris
billowing across the Galilee sky,
and know it was his funeral pyre?
The son could cling then to his mother,
but grown to man
and held only by unfeeling Roman nails,
did he find again his ancient loneliness
and hurl it into heaven?
You see what I mean?
Better to leave things buried where they lie,
or else the hurt will be too great for us to bear.
Oh, let there be dark!

There's another thing he said,
which troubles me no end:
'Father, forgive them, for they know not what
    they do.'
How can any man, or woman or child,
forgive crucifixion,
its cruelty so deliberate,
its pain so calculated?
And he was crucified as a warning,
killed for what others might do.
Is there any justice in that?
Beyond forgiveness quite.
Like John Venables.
Monster, sub-human, evil.
'He was only ten years old,' you say.
That only makes him worse,
fuels my disgust and the blaze of my anger.
I refuse to look round the edges of his crime,
to find the damaged boy,
or the man spoiled.
He is no child of God,
nor can ever be!

Let what he did blot him out!
Let there be dark,
lest I have to face the darkness in myself,
lest I have to attend to the hard work
of responding to evil with good!
If the light shines
then I will have to *do* something!
Let me be!

This is too uncomfortable by halves,
this supposed good Friday!
Give me Easter, any day,
with its chocolate eggs
and sugar-coated angels.

The geode

Hold me in your weighted hand,
lying on my back, heavy with child.
I swell like the stomach of an ancient goddess,
head, arms and legs removed,
only the place of my fertility left,
bearing the stretch marks of many labours.

And I am cut in two.

Yet what might seem my mutilation,
such monstrous surgery,
is my means of revelation.
Turn me over in your hand
and you will see.

Overturn the swelling hill of Golgotha,
dead-weighted in a world's blood-stained hands,
and you will find an empty tomb,
the piercing beauty of a wounded God.

Rebekah's story

There were women among Jesus' disciples, as all the Gospels testify. Yet their stories within those same Gospels remain largely untold. When Matthew, for example, speaks of Jesus calling James and John, the sons of Zebedee, to follow him, their mother is not mentioned. And yet later in 20.20 she suddenly appears asking Jesus for a favour for her sons, and in 27.55–56 there she is again, at Golgotha no less, a witness to Jesus' crucifixion. This is all we have (she does not appear in the other Gospels at all), so in telling her story I have had to make use of my imagination. I have had to make up a name for her, since Matthew calls her simply 'the mother of the sons of Zebedee'. Her identity in Matthew is determined by her sons and her husband. I wish to speak of her as a person in her own right.

Do you know what it's like to be invisible? You go to a party with someone, and it's as if you're not there. The one you're with is immediately surrounded by people, and you're left looking and feeling like a lemon, wondering where the drinks are, not wanting to talk to yourself because they'll notice you and think you're balmy. You don't have to be in a wheelchair, though that helps. You don't have to be a woman, or a child, though that helps, too. Or else people do notice you, but don't, if you see what I mean. They just see the wheelchair, and not the person sitting in it. 'Does he take sugar?' they say, and all that, and you say, 'I don't take sugar in wine, funnily enough, and thank you, I'll have red.' I knew a woman who was in her 80s when I first met her, though she didn't look a year over 70. Refused to tell people how old she was. We only found out when my little daughter – she was just three at the time – said to her, 'How old are you, Kitty?' 'No, how *old* are you, Kitty?' 'How old *are* you, Kitty?' and kept on at her till she told her. But you see, she didn't want people to know, because she was afraid they might not see her as Kitty any more, just an old person – 'Are you all right, dear? Can you manage, dear? Ooh, you *are* doing well for your age' – all that kind of stuff.

Me, I'm just invisible, or was then. That story about my boys mending their nets by the Sea of Galilee and Jesus calling them to follow him and them going off with him, just like that, am I in it? My husband is. Don't know why. He didn't follow Jesus. Why should he be in it, and not me? Tell you why. He's a man, isn't he – with a name that sticks in people's memories. Even got on the telly on *The Magic Roundabout* did my Zebedee. But me? Nowhere. And when I do crop up later in the story, I still don't get given a name, my name, Rebekah – not so *Magic Roundabout* as Zebedee, but a beautiful name all the same. I like it anyway.

Let me tell you how it was. My James and John weren't the only ones from our family to become followers of Jesus. It wasn't all so sudden as the story you've heard makes out either. That's just how they wrote stories like that in our day. A great teacher or prophet sees someone going about his daily business, says to them out of the blue, 'Follow me,' and they drop everything and go and are never the same again. That's how all the stories go. It wasn't like that with us. Jesus had set up home in our village, the place that smelled of fish, Capernaum. And the whole family had got to know him there and had listened to him telling his tales, his parables, and we'd all seen the way he treated people, particularly people who were having it rough for some reason. He never looked down on anyone, treated everyone the same, men, women, even children. Some of the men didn't like that. The children loved it. Some of the women weren't quite sure. Then he started talking about 'the kingdom of God', and it got more interesting still. Our family were in fishing. The Romans told us the Sea of Galilee belonged to them and everything in it. Even named it the Sea of Tiberias after the Emperor. 'Every rare and beautiful thing in the wide ocean . . . belongs to the imperial treasury,' they said. 'That's all right then,' we said, 'because the Sea of Galilee's hardly the wide ocean, just a bit of a lake. You keep the wide ocean, and we'll have the Sea of Galilee, or God will – it's his lake really, but he graciously lets us fish in it.' They didn't like that. So we had to purchase a contract with the Romans' agents to do our fishing, and we had to give them a certain quantity of fish as a tax as well, and that was hard, specially when Zebedee and the boys hadn't caught anything. The local tax collector was a man called Matthew. Not exactly a friend of ours, you might say.

So when Jesus started talking about 'the kingdom' or 'the empire' of God, we pricked our ears right up. And I mean, we. The day Jesus asked James and John to follow him, he asked me too. I wasn't mending the nets. I was with the women in the village. But James and John brought him home, and they were so excited and when he said to me, 'Will you follow me, too, Rebekah?' then what could I say? 'Of course,' I said. We were sad that Zebedee wouldn't come as well.

But Matthew did; a bit later. Matthew, the tax collector. Left it all behind and joined us. That was a shock. He was very quiet at first. Afraid he might get his throat cut in the night, I guess. But Jesus took us above all that. We all had one Father, he said, and he was God. We were all God's children. So we were all brothers and sisters, and Matthew was our brother, as simple as that. When he stopped being so quiet, we had a job stopping him.

But I still didn't really understand this kingdom of God. I thought any kingdom would be better than the Roman one, but I couldn't grasp quite how different it would be, and I thought God was like an emperor, only on a bigger throne. I'd been brought up by my parents to be a bit afraid of God. He was sort of on your side, but woe betide you if you upset him. Could come down on you like a ton of bricks and bring all sorts of disasters. He could drive the fish away and bring the nets home empty, or make your babies shake for hours with fever, or let the Romans swarm over your land with their soldiers and their rapes, their contracts and their taxes. So I learned young it was a good idea to keep on the right side of

God. I thought Jesus might do that for us, you know, tell God we weren't so bad after all. One day I had a really bright idea. I knelt in front of him, like a good little disciple, and I said, 'Jesus, could you do us a favour? Declare that these two sons of mine will sit, one at your right hand and one at your left, in your kingdom.' That should do it, I thought. With James and John all high and mighty, they'll be bound to see the family's looked after, even Zebedee, the one we left behind. They'll be able to put in a good word for us when we need it.

But Jesus said his kingdom wasn't like that, nor was our Father God. If we didn't know that already, we'd soon find out about it, he said. And we did, I tell you. There's one other place where I pop up in Matthew's story, although he still doesn't give me my name. Listen. 'Many women were also there, looking on from a distance,' his story says; 'they had followed Jesus from Galilee and had provided for him. Among them were Mary Magdalene, and Mary the mother of James and Joseph, and the mother of the sons of Zebedee.' Hear that? 'The mother of the sons of Zebedee.' That's me. Should have called me Rebekah, should Matthew, but never mind. At least he tells everyone I was there. Still there. James and John had gone into hiding in the city and were keeping their heads down. Very sensible, when your leader's just caused a rumpus in the Temple and got himself arrested, flogged and crucified. But we women didn't count with the Romans, and they didn't think we were a threat. So we were there, the three of us, as near the cross as we could get.

That was the moment when God came right out into the open. We didn't realize it at the time. It seemed in the thick darkness of crucifixion that we were as far from God as we could be, and that the kingdom Jesus had told us about was all gone. Those days up in Galilee, when he brought us such good news and made so many people well, they seemed like a dream.

Then we met him again. Oh, I know Matthew leaves me out of his story at that point, but never mind. We met him again, that's the truth, and when we did it was like meeting God, that's the truth, too. In fact, we *were* meeting God, and he still had the marks of the nails and the thorns on him. A wounded God! And all he wanted to do was hold us in his arms then wash our feet. I'd had God all wrong. There was nothing to be afraid of. I wouldn't need James and John in high places, not when God himself did the slaves' work and washed the muck off our feet.

There was one other member of the family who became a follower of Jesus that I haven't told you about. When Jesus came to Capernaum, I had a baby, little Susanna. Not mine. I was past having babies. But Sarah in the village had died having her, and then the little girl's dad died of a fever, and before we knew it the rest of the family caught it and died too. Dreadful it was, and only Susanna left. I took her in and she became mine. So when I became a follower of Jesus, Susanna came too. We became members of God's new family together, with James and John and the others. Sometimes Jesus took Susanna in his arms and said the kingdom of God belonged to her. We knew who the Roman Empire belonged to. Fancy saying the kingdom of God belonged to Susanna!

That was another thing I didn't understand till I'd been to Golgotha, seen Jesus killed and then met him again the other side of his death. I got it then.

Joanna

Joanna is mentioned by name but twice in one of the Gospels, in Luke, in 8.3 and 24.10, though given what Luke tells us in 8.1–2 her presence is also clearly implied in 23.49 and 23.55—24.9. He claims she was a witness to the crucifixion, burial and resurrection of Jesus, and unlike Matthew in the case of the mother of the sons of Zebedee, he tells us quite plainly that she was among the disciples of Jesus who followed him from place to place. This time we know what to call her, too, since Luke gives her a name, and the information he gives us in 8.1–3 is enough to place her in the Jewish aristocracy and to suggest she was wealthy. Luke says Jesus healed her, though he goes into no detail about her illness. Richard Bauckham devotes to her a long chapter of his book Gospel Women: Studies of the Named Women in the Gospels *(T&T Clark, 2002), and my piece is much indebted to his work, though I have made use of my own imagination a good deal. In particular Bauckham lays out the case for identifying Joanna with the Apostle Junia, mentioned by Paul in Romans 16.7. He is careful to point out the arguments are not conclusive, but I have gratefully made use of them.*

Have you ever been to the Sea of Galilee? It's a most beautiful place. 'The Sea of Kingfishers' I call it. It's full of them. The black and white ones hover over the water, their sharp eyes searching for fish, then fold their wings and disappear beneath the surface, to emerge less than a moment later with shining silver held tight in their bills, to be twisted and tipped down their throats.

I'd spent many an hour watching them from the garden of our house at Tiberias. It was one of the grandest houses in the city, with its gardens running down to the water. My husband, Chuza, was Herod Antipas' finance minister. He'd been responsible for raising the money to build Tiberias, and Sepphoris and Livias, too. Tiberias was Herod's capital. My husband and I were important members of his court. I changed my Hebrew name to the Latin Junia. It fitted in better. My husband had large estates, and I was a wealthy woman in my own right, with money given to me by my father when I married.

I lived a world away from Nazareth, and we all despised the peasants of villages like that. They were useful to us, because they paid their taxes, but otherwise they didn't count. We kept well clear of them, and they of us. They hated us. Tiberias was a blot on their landscape, flaunting its wealth and power, reminding them all the time they had neither. It was founded on their taxes, and we still lived off them, taxes harsh enough for them in good years, and many years were not good at all. Drought, locusts or disease went round the villages too often.

But the high walls of Tiberias couldn't keep disease out. I got sick, an infection in one of my feet. The doctors in the city could do nothing for me, and that's when I met Jesus. Ruth, one of my slave-girls, took me to him. She'd got in with some of the fishermen from further up the lake, and they'd introduced her to him. We'd all heard stories about him, some of them very alarming. All sorts of riff-raff were going round with him. He was always on the move, in one village after another, speaking of a kingdom of God, where the first were last and the last were first. We in Tiberias were the first, and we did not want to be last, thank you very much. We knew too much about what being last meant. And we didn't want peasants or worse thinking they were first either. Herod had stopped John the Baptist in his tracks, because he'd become dangerously popular. It wouldn't be long, we thought, before he would have to take action against this Jesus, too.

Then I met him. Ruth took me a few miles along the shore of the lake, to where he was having a meal with his friends. Each lurch of the ass was agony for me, and I collapsed at his feet. I must have fainted. When I came to, he was washing my feet, both of them, as my slave-girls did, and the pain was gone! After that he sat me down among his friends and gave me some bread, fish and wine. It was the first time in my life I'd eaten a meal sitting on the ground, and I'd never eaten with men and children before, or with people of such poverty or notoriety. And the wine I was used to had always come from abroad, not like theirs. But it was the best wine I'd ever tasted.

And they didn't hate me! They knew who I was. Ruth had told them. But they didn't hate me. They didn't defer to me either, of course. Not like the people in the court at Tiberias, who were generally so sycophantic, hoping to keep on the right side of my husband. Jesus didn't defer to me, yet in his company I felt the most important person on God's earth. I could see all the others felt the same, including Ruth. I'd never felt so free, never been so free.

So we joined his circle, Ruth and I. Astonishing thing to do, for me at least, but we could do no other. I left Tiberias, left the court and our grand house and its gardens by the water, left my husband for the time being, took up again my old Hebrew name Yohannah, and brought my money with me, to buy food for us all and help keep us alive.

Ruth and I were right beside him as he rode into Jerusalem just before Passover and caused such chaos in the Temple. He was arrested, of course. The men disappeared, went to safe houses in the nearby villages, but we women disciples stuck around. The authorities didn't bother about us, thought we weren't a threat. I'd got friends in high places in the city, and they informed us Jesus had been sentenced to death by crucifixion and told us the spot chosen for the execution and the time set for it.

I'd heard about crucifixion, of course, but I'd never seen someone crucified before.

Afterwards we watched him being buried. They were in a hurry and didn't have time to do it properly, so we came back after the Sabbath. I'd managed to get some spices from one of my friends. We meant to wash his body, anoint him to replace the smell of death, and say prayers over him. But our spices were unnecessary, for when we got there, we found ourselves in heaven! Without realizing it, we'd stepped into the circle of the divine. We were in a strange world, where large stones at the doors of tombs are swept away like dead leaves, where death doesn't hold sway any more and the air rustles to the sound of angels' wings instead; a world of eternal spring, where righteousness and peace have kissed each other and faithfulness has sprung up from the ground, where the leopard lies down with the kid, the calf and the lion and the fatling together and a little child is in charge of them all; a world where the old centres of human power count for nothing, where those who have denied and deserted take their place again in the circle and sit and eat; a world where old hopes are renewed, and new ones, undreamed of, are born; a world of good news, where all the world's ills and its blessings are put into new perspective.

It was utterly wonderful, beyond the finest words! We hurried straightaway to tell the others. They were still in hiding, but they needed to be together and so were all in one house. We tried to tell them of the new world we'd found, and we explained he wasn't in the tomb; there was no corpse, we said, not even the smell of one left behind. The men wouldn't believe us at first. We'd returned, it seemed, to the old world, where women weren't to be believed and their witness wasn't to be trusted. We were so excited and of course we weren't entirely coherent. How can you be coherent when you've just stumbled upon the divine? But their dismissing what we said as idle chatter took the wind right out of our sails. It was as if Jesus had never been. He'd never treated women like that, never treated us like that. They'd seen that for themselves, and in his presence they'd overcome their prejudice. Now he was gone, it was as if they'd turned back to how they were at the start of it all. 'But he's not gone!' we cried, and they said, 'We thought you just said he was,' and we had nothing more to say.

Peter believed us, at least enough to go back to the tomb. He saw something there of what we'd discovered, but came back more bewildered than us. We'd begun to see everything in a new light. Poor Peter was simply dazzled by it.

We all found the truth in the end, though, even Chuza, my husband, whom I'd left behind in Tiberias. He was in Jerusalem for the Passover, you see, and we managed to meet up again. He was with us that day, with those of us who'd been with Jesus in Galilee, when suddenly we all heard God's footsteps. He'd come once more to join our circle and share our hospitality. He was at once strange and familiar. God is always strange, beyond our expecting, but this God we'd known in Galilee and we'd followed him to Jerusalem! I'd seen him fighting for his life, seen him dead and buried, I thought. But God was not dead! God was not dead, though it seemed he was marked with the scars of crucifixion.

So began a new life for me and Chuza. I'd had a new beginning already back in Galilee, but I hadn't fully grasped its meaning. I'd thought it was only for Galilee, for Judea, for the Jewish people, and a few Gentiles who came for the warmth of Jesus' embrace. Now we knew we must take the death-defeating, scarred, limping God of ours to a wider world. They needed people to go to Rome, because Jewish pilgrims from there had heard some of us preaching in Jerusalem and had returned home wanting more. Chuza and I would know our way round Rome. We had old contacts there. So the leaders of the Jerusalem church sent us. I picked up my Latin name again, Junia, and Chuza became Andronicus, and those are the names Paul knew us by. Ruth didn't come with us. She wasn't my slave any more, of course, and she had her own work to do. But all that's another story. This one is enough for now.

Remember. God is not dead. But he does now walk with a limp. Don't go back to your old ways, like the men did. Go on with him to new things.

Ruth

For the story 'Joanna' I invented a slave girl called Ruth. This is her tale. While Luke does not tell of her, he does refer to 'many other women' among Jesus' disciples when first he mentions Joanna in 8.3, and again in 24.10, when he speaks of her a second time, he talks of 'the other women' with her. I have placed Ruth in their company. The Ruth of the story in the Old Testament that bears her name is an outsider, a Moabite, as characters in the story and the narrator remind us many times, and most of the action takes place in Bethlehem. This tale also begins in Bethlehem and I have portrayed Ruth as a Bedouin.

Luke has me down as one of the 'other women'. Somewhere along the way I lost my name, it seems. Ruth. I lost my husband and my children, too. My husband, Ishmael, was one of the first of Jesus' disciples. Became one when Jesus was just a baby; saw him in a manger in Bethlehem. Came back to our tents smelling of angels, saying he'd looked into the face of God. He was a changed man after that. Treated me quite differently.

We didn't live in Bethlehem. We didn't live in any village. We were nomads, living out in the open. That's where the angels found my Ishmael, and the other men. We weren't particularly popular. Good pasture was scarce and the villagers wanted it for their own flocks. So we moved on, and eventually found ourselves up in Galilee. Or I did. Ishmael caught a fever on the way, so did the children, and one after another they all died. I stayed with the tribe, of course, but then we got into serious trouble with the shepherds on Joanna's estates. Several of our men were injured, before Joanna herself intervened.

She needed another woman slave at the time. One of hers had just died. My people sold me to her, well, gave me to her, as a matter of fact. I was not much use to them any more, and I became part of the bargain, the deal they struck with her to let them pasture their flocks in a corner of her land.

Soon after that she became sick and I looked after her. There wasn't much I could do for her. I hadn't been able to do anything for my husband or my children, and I was just as helpless with my mistress. It looked to me as though she was going to die as well. Then everything changed, for both of us. I heard of a healer in the area, and I took her to see him. She didn't want to go. 'He's from Nazareth,' she said. 'Can anything good come out of Nazareth?' But she was too weak to argue. So we went. And we never came back. When he said 'Follow me', no one could have stopped us.

We joined his circle, along with Mary from Magdala and Susanna. They were rich, like Joanna. Had money of their own to play with. I had nothing, of course. But it made no difference

with him whether you had anything or not. There were fishermen with him, and a tax collector as well, the one who'd been
fleecing the fishermen and making their lives a misery, and
street children, and us women. Made no difference who you
were. We were all children of God, he said, and that was the
only thing that mattered. I wasn't Joanna's slave any more. I
wasn't anyone's slave. God didn't have slaves, he said. We were
family, he said, all of us. He treated me just like the rest, and
the rest just like me.

He made up a story about me once. I'd lost one of the coins
from my headdress and gone frantic looking for it. It was one
of the few things I still had to remind me of my tribe and my
husband and my children. I found it eventually, and I was so
overjoyed I took all the coins and used them to buy a goat so
we could have a party. Jesus laughed his head off and said it
was just the kind of thing God would do, and promptly turned
me into a parable.

Joanna and I were completely devoted to him, remained so
right to the end. We were among those who watched him die.
It was as if God died with him, and the world was left empty
of all meaning.

We followed Joseph of Arimathea and saw the posh tomb
where he laid Jesus' body. Joanna knew some of the families
who had tombs next to his, really rich people like her. But they
didn't have time to do the burial properly, what with the Sabbath
coming on. There was just time to put his body inside and roll
the stone across the entrance before the sun set. So after the
Sabbath was over, we went back there. Joanna and Mary had
bought some expensive spices and perfumes and divided them
between us. But we came out of that tomb smelling of angels
instead, just like my husband all those years before.

You see, there was no corpse for us to attend to. Terrifying
that was at first. I thought the tomb must have been robbed,
but Joanna said one of the rich families who owned one of the
nearby tombs must have objected to having a peasant from

Galilee, a condemned criminal at that, being buried next to their ancestors. 'They'll have thrown him on a rubbish heap,' she said. We went back outside into the dazzling early morning sun, and suddenly an angel of the Lord stood before us and a multitude of the heavenly host surrounded us praising God. We took off our shoes at once; we were on holy ground.

But I still thought we'd come too late. We'd missed him and only found the angels he'd left behind. You can't complain when you meet angels, I suppose, but I couldn't help thinking of the story Ishmael had told me those many years before, when angels had led him to a manger in Bethlehem. The angels had been only the beginning, he'd said, and the end had been beyond all expectation. He'd looked into the eyes of God. That's what he'd told me. So when the angels said, 'He's not here,' I was disappointed. I wanted to see what Ishmael had seen. But Joanna and Mary said, 'Come on, we must tell the others!' I said, 'But what shall we tell them?' 'That it all makes sense,' they replied. 'That God's not dead after all.' 'Well, I could have told you that!' I said.

We ran back into the city and went to the house where our friends were hiding together and told them everything. They didn't believe us. 'You're being hysterical,' the men said.

In that dreadful moment it was as if he'd never been. Men said that women were unreliable on the subject of God, that God dealt with men and sensibly kept women out of it. We women had all grown up surrounded by attitudes like that. 'Look at Abraham and Sarah,' they said, 'or Moses and Miriam. God doesn't know how to speak to women.' But Jesus had never said that. He'd gone wild when anyone said that kind of thing. We were children of God, he said, and that was all that mattered. He'd washed *our* feet, too.

We'd all gone through so much with him. I thought we all saw things as he did, felt things as he did. I thought he'd become a part of us. I thought we'd all been changed, at the deepest level. And now the men seemed to have gone straight back to their old ways, and were treating us women as fools. We were their friends! We were family! Was it because we'd stuck with him right through crucifixion and burial, and had gone back with our spices when they'd fled and stayed in hiding? Did we remind them of their shame, and so they were taking it out on us?

Perhaps so, but whatever the reason, we couldn't stay in that room any longer. We opened the door and fled.

We fell straight into the arms of God.

That's the only way I can describe it. Luke doesn't tell the story, but everyone knows we women were the first to meet him, the risen Jesus.

God is not only far beyond us. He's also warm, and close, and very familiar. When we fell into his arms, we recognized the embrace at once.

I knew then what my Ishmael had been talking about all those years before, when he and the others came back from Bethlehem.

The breaking of bread

A reflection on the famous story of 'the walk to Emmaus' in Luke 24.13–35, in which the risen Jesus joins two of his disciples as they return to their home after the crucifixion. Luke only names one of them, Cleopas, but presumably the other is his wife. At least, that is the most natural assumption to make, and it is the one we adopt here.

It was a beautiful afternoon, when we set out to walk to Emmaus. We didn't see it, nor did we feel the warmth of the sun, but shivered in the cold of our grief and bewilderment. I guess we were still in shock.

I'd been there, at Golgotha, seen him crucified, watched the slow agony of his dying. Cleopas, my husband, had gone into hiding. So we each had our terrible burden of memory to bear.

My head was full of images of his pain and his fighting for breath. Cleopas was crushed by guilt. Like the other men he'd deserted him in the hour of his greatest need. And why? So he could save his own skin, he said. I kept telling him he'd had no choice, what with the Romans and the Temple police. A few of us women had been able to join the crowd taking him to Golgotha and been able to escape notice, but the men would have been arrested almost certainly, or attacked.

I said all this to Cleopas, but it didn't make any difference. He couldn't break out of his guilt and sense of failure. He still couldn't, even when some of the women came running back from Jesus' tomb crying it was full of heaven. They'd seen angels, they said, who'd told them death hadn't been strong enough to hold him. He was alive with the life of God, they said. The men told them they were being hysterical. Peter and a few others ran off to the tomb, it's true, and came back saying the women were right, the tomb was empty. But that's all the news they had, nothing about angels or heaven. They didn't know what to think, they said.

Nor did we. We couldn't bear to stay in that room. Most of them were sunk in blank despair, while the women who'd found the tomb were left huddled in a corner. They'd found the truth – we soon found that out – but they were being treated like idiots. They knew why, as well, and that only made it worse. The others didn't believe them because they were women.

It made me weep. 'Come on,' I said to Cleopas, 'we're going home. I can't stand it here.'

We were cold inside, cold as death. The sun didn't warm us on our journey.

He came to us as we walked and disturbed our grief. His feet made no sound, but we didn't notice. He hobbled along as though his feet had been hurt, but we thought nothing of it. He smelled of heaven, but we were oblivious to it. You would have thought we would have recognized his voice, but it was as if it came from another world. We told him everything that had happened. Just imagine it! He'd been at the centre of it all, and there we were, telling him the whole story! He was our friend, our teacher, our healer and companion, and we were speaking to him as if we'd never met him. Of course, he was used to his friends saying they never knew him. Peter hadn't been the only one, just the one who'd been brave enough to own up to it.

He was our Lord and our God, too. Were we utterly over-whelmed? Not a bit! But then we forget how self-effacing our God is and how full of surprises. We miss him all the time.

Yet gradually this stranger warmed us and brought us back to life. He was intriguing, inviting. It was getting towards dusk by the time we reached home, so of course we asked him to eat with us and rest the night in our house. He took some persuading. He didn't want to be any trouble, he said, and we said it would be an honour for us. We didn't know what we were saying, of course. We thought we were simply being courteous, in the usual way, and honest. We really didn't want to let him go, nor leave him out in the cold. We said we hoped he would forgive our small house and the plainness of our food. It was what he was used to, he said, and smiled. At that a flash of recognition went through my head, as if there was a familiarity about him that I couldn't put my finger on.

I prepared the meal and put it in front of him and Cleopas. Then something very odd happened. He took the bread and said the prayer of blessing over it. That was Cleopas' job, and if any other guest had done it, we would have felt deeply insulted. But we didn't. Instead, it was as though he was making our hospitality holy. And then, and this was the oddest thing of all, he broke the bread into three equal pieces and gave one to each of us. That was *my* job! But I didn't feel pushed aside. It was as if he were my servant, waiting upon me, and Cleopas, too.

We didn't have any slaves; we'd never had anyone to wait upon us, either of us. At least, we had, just one person, Jesus of Nazareth. When we joined him and ate with him and his other followers, we found he would take the bread, bless it, break it and divide it between us. None of us had ever seen anything like that, whether we were women or men. He did the woman's work as well as the man's. He washed our feet, too. That was even harder to take, because that was the work not just of a woman, but of a woman slave and the lowest of the lot. But he did it. It was his trademark, that and breaking and dividing the bread at meals. Once we accepted it and didn't fight against what he was doing, we felt like royalty. No, we felt like *family*, like precious sons and daughters, and when he taught us to call God 'Abba', we all knew whose family we belonged to.

That's why all of a sudden we recognized him when he broke the bread. He was doing the woman's work, too! We sprang up, but he was gone. We knew we didn't have our old friend back. We had much more than that. In our small house, in the simplicity of that simple meal, we'd found God, seen Abba. He'd walked with us, become our companion on our journey home, and then he'd bent his head to come through our door and share our hospitality, as if he needed it, as if we'd saved him from the darkness and hunger of the night.

And that's why he'd walked with such difficulty, and why we saw in his hands, as he handed the bread to us, marks left behind by nails. He was a God who'd been through crucifixion.

It wasn't the last time we ate with him. We quickly rejoined the others, of course, back in Jerusalem, and in the weeks, months and years after that we would come together in one another's houses, and we would wash one another's feet and take it in turns, men, women and children, to take the bread, bless it, break it and pass it round. Whenever we did that, it was as if he was there. In fact, he *was* there. Even those who'd never known him in Galilee or Jerusalem met him in those meals we shared together.

We see things differently now. Everyone's a member of God's family, everyone, no one's excluded, no one's put down, no one's cast out. That's what he was teaching us in Galilee and Jerusalem, and on Golgotha especially. He didn't do the woman's work just to make us women feel good. He did it because he wanted the men to give us as much honour as they gave themselves, and all of us to treat everyone the same. He didn't just do the work of the lowest slave to make us feel appropriately humbled. He wanted to show us another world, where the first were last and the last were first. He wanted us to recognize that world for what it was, the household of God, and then he wanted us to join him as his retinue in making that world a reality. He gave us a job to do, the hardest and most prestigious job anyone could ask for.

We couldn't refuse him.

Teaching God to dance

The greatest of all the resurrection stories in the four Gospels is the one in John 20 of Mary of Magdala's meeting with the risen Jesus. This reflection on that story, the last of the Easter pieces in this collection, appeared in my book The Easter Stories. *Its beginning is taken from my imagination, though Luke tells us that Jesus had healed Mary from a very serious illness.*

When I was a girl in Magdala my mother told me ancient stories of God and my people, the Jews. One began like this: 'And it happened after these things that God tested Abraham. And he said to him, "Abraham!" and he said, "Here I am." And he said, "Take, pray, your son, your only one, whom you love, Isaac . . . and offer him up as a burnt offering . . ."'

I hated that story. I thought its God was a monster. 'What about Sarah?' I asked my mother. 'Did God ask her to go as well?'

'No,' my mother replied.

'Why not?'

'Because . . . You will learn why in due time, Mary.'

'You mean it was because she was a woman and women don't count.'

'You are too old for your years, Mary,' my mother said.

Another night she told me the story of Moses and the burning bush. 'Only a bush?' I said. 'Not a great tree? I thought gods had sacred trees, not bushes. Does that mean our God was not big enough to have a tree, only a stupid bush?'

My mother looked at me. 'Only the God of all the universe would be content with a bush,' she replied.

I may have been too old for my years, but I didn't understand that.

'And God called to him', she continued, 'from the midst of the bush, and said, "Moses, Moses!" And he said, "Here I am." Then he said, "Come no closer here. Take off your sandals from your feet, for the place you are standing on is holy ground."'

'But Moses was married to Zipporah at the time,' I interrupted. 'Tell me a story about God saying to Zipporah, "Zipporah, Zipporah!"'

'There isn't one,' my mother said.

'Might've guessed,' I said.

When it came to the story of the boy Samuel, and God waking him in the night over and over with his 'Samuel, Samuel!' I'd had enough. 'I don't want to know,' I said.

When I grew up and started my periods and got married to a rich man with lots of slaves and animals and barns not big enough for his harvests, I learned afresh that women didn't count. He hit me on our wedding night. He hit me every night. And every night he raped me. There's no other word for it. And when, to my despair, I found myself pregnant with his child and couldn't hide it from him any more, he shouted, 'Why didn't you tell me? Are you ashamed of it? It's a girl, is it? Is that it? A filth of a girl curled up inside you! Well, we'll see about that!' And he kicked me in the stomach and kept kicking me until he'd finished and the child inside me was dead.

He divorced me after that. Because I couldn't have children any more and was incapable of giving him a son.

And that is why, when Jesus came to Magdala, he found me mad. My family were ashamed of me and had shut me in a small, windowless room, never allowing me out. They even gave up using my name. I crouched in the corner of that room, swaying back and forth. Or else I danced, a slow, awkward, gangly dance, that got faster and faster, until I would fall on the floor exhausted. Jesus of Nazareth found me in that room. I was dancing. 'Don't touch me!' I shouted. He waited and waited, waited till I fell in a heap at his feet. 'Mary!' he said. And then, after a long pause, and very quietly, 'Follow me.'

And so I did, of course. From village to village, to city, to grand temple, to crucifixion, to death, to burial.

Then there was nothing I could do for him any more. Except dance. That is why I went to the tomb, to dance for him outside. He wouldn't be able to see, of course. The stone would be between us, and in any case he was dead. But I would dance and dance and dance, until I fell exhausted to the ground, and then I would hope for death to come to me, too, so we could be together, him and me.

But he wasn't in the tomb. It was full of angels instead. No room for him. I was in a different world. Somewhere along the path through the garden I'd crossed the line between earth and heaven, between the empire of Tiberius and the kingdom of God. But I hadn't seen it. It was still dark, I suppose, though that seems a feeble excuse. I was blind with grief. That's a better one, I guess. In this new world of God, dead bodies were replaced by angels. Only I didn't want angels. I wanted him.

'They've taken him away!' I cried. I didn't know who 'they' were, but they must have put him somewhere and I wanted to find out, so I could go and pick him up and hold him in my arms, as once, in that small, dark, fetid room in Magdala, he had held me till my madness had gone and I had found my sanity. 'Mary!' he had said. Now I would hold him and call his name over and over, and it would do no good, but I'd be able to say there was nothing more I could have done and try one day to kid myself out of grief.

But he wasn't there. At some point I'd crossed over into the kingdom of God, but I didn't know it. I'd met angels, for God's sake, but still I didn't realize where I was! I thought I was in the world where people could take bodies out of tombs too posh for them and dump them on the rubbish heap, and where men beat their wives and kicked the foetuses out of them. I didn't really notice the angels. At least, I did, but it didn't sink in. I panicked, you see. All I wanted was him, to dance for him, to hold him, for one last time.

Something made me turn round. I thought he was the gardener. I asked him whether he had taken Jesus away. Why in heaven's name would a gardener do such a thing? I wasn't thinking straight. Grief's like that, of course. You think silly things and sometimes you say them out loud.

'Mary!' he said.

'Here I am,' I replied.

I went to embrace him, to hold him, as once he had held me. But you can't get your arms round God. So I took off my sandals for the dance instead. I held out my hands to him.

'I cannot dance,' he said. 'The nails,' he said. 'You have a limping God now, Mary.'

'Then I will teach you a limping dance,' I replied. 'Once you were my teacher. You taught me how to dance. Not that jagged, exhausting dance of my madness and my rage, but the dance of your very particular kind of sanity. "The Dance of the Kingdom of God" you called it. Now I will be your teacher, and after we have done, then I will wash your feet. You taught me how to do that, too.'

And that is how I taught my God to dance.

4

Treasures of the Old Testament

---•◦•---

Sarah

*Even in an English translation we can see that Genesis 22's story
of the Binding of Isaac is one of the most beautifully crafted and
powerful stories in the Bible. Yet its theology is highly problematic,
and there are two other things about it that are strange and mighty
disconcerting: Abraham's initial silence and Sarah's absence. The
prayer of lament and complaint bulks large in the Old Testament,
and is famous for its candour and forcefulness. Yet when God tells
Abraham to go to the land of Moriah and there sacrifice his son
as a burnt offering, he sets off without a murmur. More shocking
still is that Abraham's wife, Isaac's mother, Sarah, does not appear
in the story at all. (And yet, as Genesis 21 makes plain, it is she who
is so attached to Isaac, and so she, by the terms of Genesis 22,
who needs to be tested by God.) Genesis 22.2–3 goes like this: God
said to Abraham, '"Take your son, your only son Isaac, whom you
love, and go to the land of Moriah, and offer him there as a burnt-
offering on one of the mountains that I shall show you." So
Abraham rose early in the morning, saddled his donkey, and took
two of his young men with him, and his son Isaac; he cut the wood
for the burnt-offering, and set out . . .' Substitute the name Sarah
for Abraham there, and at once it becomes impossible.*

*Two more things before we begin: the rabbis long ago noted
that the end of the story in Genesis 22 speaks of Abraham going
back home with his young men, but does not mention Isaac, while
Genesis 23 opens with a report of Sarah's death. They concluded*

that she died of a broken heart, when Isaac did not return with his father. (With profound and wonderful irony Genesis 24.62 tells of Isaac settling in the Negev desert, at Beer-lahai-roi. Beer-lahai-roi is the place where the Egyptian Hagar, pregnant with Abraham's first child, meets with God in Genesis 16, having run away from her mistress, Sarah.) Second, Abraham's vision in the second part of my piece is taken not from the Bible, but from my imagination, though for much of its detail it draws upon the story in Genesis 18 of God's visit to Abraham.

She had been watching out for them for days. It was the hottest part of the day and her eyes were heavy. But this time, when she opened them again, she saw them coming. She jumped up and ran to meet them.

'Where have you been?' she cried. 'And where's Isaac?'

She had not embraced her husband. There could be no embrace without Isaac. The two young slaves stood by the donkey looking at the ground.

'Where's Isaac?' she repeated.

'I'm tired and hungry, and my feet are sore,' Abraham replied. 'Fetch some water and wash my feet, and then go and cook me a meal.'

'Where is Isaac?' she said a third time, the panic rising in her voice.

'I don't know.'

'You don't know! What do you mean, you don't know?'

'He went his own way, in the direction of Hagar's well. If you go there, you might find him.'

Sarah was utterly bewildered. 'I don't begin to understand you,' she said. 'You're talking gibberish. All I know is you set out with Isaac and these two slaves nearly a week ago, early, before I was awake. And now you tell me you don't know where Isaac is, but he might be at the well of that Egyptian slut. I don't understand. I don't understand any of it. You left without a word to me. One of my slaves saw you go. Said you left with a pile of wood and fire and the special knife, as if you were going to offer a sacrifice. That's all I know. Where is Isaac?'

'We went to the land of Moriah.'

'To Moriah? For God's sake, why?'

'There's a holy mountain there. At least, there is now.'

'These sacred oaks here at Mamre weren't good enough for you?'

Abraham said nothing.

'Tell me one thing,' she persisted. 'My slave said you took no animal with you for the sacrifice. Unless you were intending to slaughter the donkey!' She looked across to where the slaves were standing, the donkey still beside them. Their eyes remained fixed on the ground. 'But that makes no sense. You set off with all the trappings for sacrifice, and no animal. The whole point is you must take an animal from your own flock or herd, or the thing's a sham. Did you steal someone else's ewe lamb along the way and offer that to God as your own? Or did you catch a ram caught in a thicket by its horns?' She laughed.

'I caught a ram, trapped in a thicket, just as you said.'

'What?'

'A ram caught in a thicket by its horns.'

'What do you mean? And where in heaven's name is Isaac?'

Abraham sighed, then continued in a dry, mechanical voice: 'God told me to take him to the land of Moriah, to a mountain he would show me, and offer him there as a sacrifice, a burnt offering. So when we got there, I loaded the wood for his sacrifice onto his back, while I carried the fire and the knife, and we climbed the mountain together, to the very top, and I built an altar there, and bound him up, and put him on top of the altar – the slaves were waiting with the donkey at the bottom – and I took the knife in my hand, and I was just about to . . . when God spoke to me and showed me a ram held in a thicket by its horns and told me to sacrifice it.'

Sarah was trembling violently, her eyes wild, her skin the colour of death, her tongue stuck in her throat. From somewhere outside herself she found enough voice to speak again. 'So when you set out that morning,' she said, 'with the wood, the fire and the knife, you were meaning to sacrifice my son, my only son, the one I love, Isaac?'

'Yes.'

'For God's sake, why?'

'Because God told me to.'

'Because God told you to! Did you protest at all? Did you ask him what the hell he was playing at?'

'No.'

'So you just went? You got up before the crack of dawn and took my son?'

'Yes.'

Yet more horror suddenly came over Sarah's face. Very quietly, the words barely audible, she asked, 'Did you sacrifice him with the ram?'

'No, I did not. I untied him. But he ran off. In the direction of Hagar's well. I couldn't follow. He was too quick for me, and I had to get back to the slaves and the donkey.'

Sarah put her hands to her head. 'You stupid, stupid, stupid old man!' she cried. She turned and walked away. She went beyond the circle of shade cast by the sacred oaks, out into the cruel heat of the sun.

Abraham watched her, his wife, a tiny, bent old woman, staring into the sun, shaking her fist at the heavens. She was shouting something, but he was too far away to hear what it was. Then suddenly he saw her body crumple and fall to the ground. She looked no more than a heap of discarded clothes.

The slaves ran over to her, and Abraham followed them as fast as he could, but it was too late.

Abraham was old, full of age to the very brim. He was sitting at the entrance to his tent in the heat of the day. His eyes closed and his chin dropped onto his chest. Then it was, after so many years, he had a dream.

He saw Sarah coming towards him, no longer bent, but with her head held high, her hair the shining black of her youth. She looked every inch a princess, and suddenly, as if for the first time, he loved her, and in his sleep he called out her name. He sprang up, as if he too were young again, ran from the tent entrance to meet her and bowed himself low to the ground.

'My lady,' he cried, 'if I find favour with you, do not pass by your servant. I will fetch water from the well, and I will wash your feet, Sarah, for the first time, Sarah, and you can rest in the shade of the trees here, for you have been out in the burning sun far too long, and I will bring you some bread and cook you a pile of cakes, like the ones you used to make, and I will kill a fatted calf, tender and good, and bring curds and milk, and together we will fill this place with laughter, Sarah, my darling Sarah.'

He held out his arms.

When Isaac and Ishmael found him, Abraham's face was cold, wet with a woman's tears. They buried him in the cave of Machpelah, in the field of Ephron, east of Mamre, beside his wife Sarah.

A boy is born

With extraordinary and most tragic irony the story of the people of God in the Old Testament begins with a determination to wipe them off the face of the earth, not by herding them into gas chambers and shovelling them into crematoria, but by the killing of their boy babies at birth. (Genesis is concerned with their ancestors, but is a tale of a family that does not become a people till the start of Exodus.) Moses is caught up in that attempted genocide, and this piece is a reflection on the story of his birth and his escape in Exodus 2.1–10. That story is almost wholly concerned with women: Moses' mother (named Jochebed in Exodus 6.20), his sister (called Miriam in Exodus 15.20–21 and in Numbers 26.59), and the daughter of the Pharaoh and her slave-girls. After verse 1 they are responsible for all the action and for everything that is said (all that Moses does, understandably, is lie there and cry). In this important respect, Luke's stories of the birth of Jesus, where Mary and Elizabeth play such prominent roles, remind us more clearly of the Exodus passage than Matthew. Yet Moses' birth is surrounded by fear and the threat of the slaughter of babies at the command of a brutal, paranoid tyrant. That makes us think at once of Herod in Matthew's story of the visit of the magi to the newborn Jesus, and of his slaughter of the infants of Bethlehem (Matthew 2.1–18).

There is one interesting omission in Exodus 2. There is no mention of Aaron, who is spoken of as Moses' brother only two chapters later, in 4.14, and in Exodus 7.7 is described as being three years older than him. In my retelling of the story I have respected its limits and kept its silence on the matter. One change I have made: the stories of the early chapters of Exodus speak of the people of Israel as 'Hebrews'; I call them 'Jews'. An echo of Genesis I have carefully preserved. The Hebrew word for the floating 'basket' made for Moses, as it is usually called in English translations, is the same as the one used in the Flood story for Noah's 'ark'. Beyond these two stories it does not appear anywhere in the Old Testament.

I have put the words of my piece in the mouth of Jochebed, Moses' mother.

It began with pain and fear. The pain of his birth was bad enough, and the wondering whether the pushing would get you anywhere, and whether either of you would survive. But they were soon forgotten. It's so hard at the time, and you don't know whether it's ever going to end, but when you have the baby in your arms, you forget all that.

But the trouble was we were living in the wrong place at the wrong time. No promised land for us, but an Egyptian labour camp, and a tyrant of a Pharaoh who wanted rid of us. We Jews were different. We didn't fit, we didn't belong. He even saw us as a threat to the security of his country. He tried forced labour first, and when that didn't break us, he decided to use midwives. He ordered them to kill our boy babies at birth. But he failed to reckon with the midwives' courage. They flatly refused to obey his orders. Didn't tell him, of course, just got on with their job, safely delivering mothers of their babies, whether they were girls or boys. Pharaoh's informers told him what they were doing, of course, or what they were *not* doing, and he went mad. He summoned them to his palace. None of us thought we would ever see them again, but they told him we all had our babies so quick they could never get there on time. And he believed them! He gave up on midwives after that. But he didn't give up on his plan. If the midwives couldn't kill the babies, his own people would have to do it. He issued them with a decree: 'Whenever a Jewish woman has a baby boy,' it said, 'get him and fling him into the Nile.' Well, that was clear.

That's why, when I had Moses and the midwife said it was a boy, we all went quiet. Pharaoh had his men patrolling the alleyways between the huts, listening for babies crying. They would threaten our women who went to the well, ordering them to tell them who was expecting and when it was due. No one had told them about me, thank God, and the midwife had escaped their attention. But when the baby cried, we were all petrified, including Miriam.

We held him tight and tried to comfort him as best we could, but babies cry, it's what they do. And they pick up your mood, of course. Moses knew we were frightened. He could tell from the way we held him, from the tone of our voices and the look in our eyes. So he got frightened himself, and that opened his lungs wide. They're so small, are newborn babies, but the noise they make isn't. I fed him as soon as he was hungry, and fortunately my milk came quickly. I lay awake in the night listening to his breathing beside me, waiting for him to stir, putting him to the breast as soon as he did. But that tired me out, and one day I fell into a deep sleep. Amram, my husband, was out working, and Miriam had gone to the well. Moses started crying for milk, and I didn't hear him. Next thing I knew, Miriam was shaking me. She was holding Moses crying in her arms. As soon as he was feeding, he quietened down, but we huddled together the three of us, and Miriam and I waited for Pharaoh's men to burst through the door.

Thank God, they didn't come, but we realized we couldn't keep him in the hut any longer. It wasn't safe. Nowhere was safe, but the river would be the best place, we thought. If Pharaoh said the babies should be put in the Nile, so be it. We'd put Moses in the Nile. Only we'd make him a little boat, a kind of ark, like Noah's only smaller, and we'd make it watertight and we'd put a lid on it and hide it among the reeds along the river's edge, and Miriam could keep an eye on him, and if he cried, then she'd run and fetch me, and I'd go and look after him and put him back, once he'd settled.

'It might work,' we said, but only Miriam thought it would. Amram and I, we knew he'd be found sooner or later. But what else could we do?

So I made the ark and we put him inside, with the toy camel Miriam had made for him, and we hid him among the reeds when no one was looking, and I went home, while Miriam kept watch.

We kept it up for over a week. Then one day Moses started crying and Miriam couldn't run to fetch me, because Pharaoh's daughter was there, with her slave-girls. The princess had come to the river to bathe, and she was right by the place where the little ark was, when he began to cry. She looked down, saw the ark and told one of her slaves to fetch it out of the water. She opened the lid, and there he was, our Moses, looking up at her and bawling for milk. Miriam heard what she said. 'Well I never!' she exclaimed. 'A little Jewish boy!'

Miriam's heart was in her mouth. It was bad enough to have anyone find him. Pharaoh had his informants even among us Jews. But Pharaoh's own daughter! Her father was the one who'd given the order for the babies to be drowned. Miriam thought she would take Moses out by the heels and fling him as far as she could across the water. She did take him out, not by the heels, though, but gently, and then she was cuddling him and rocking him and putting her finger into his mouth, to give him something to suck, so he would stop crying.

It didn't work for long, of course. So Miriam came out from where she'd been hiding and ran straight up to the princess, bold as anything, and asked if she could go and fetch someone to nurse the baby and give him some milk. 'He'll stop crying then,' she said. 'Thank you. That's a good idea,' the princess said. Would you believe it? So Miriam ran as fast as she could, and came back with *me*! The princess handed Moses to me, and he quietened down as soon as I started feeding him, and she said, Pharaoh's daughter did, would I look after him and she would pay me for the trouble! I wanted to hug her, only I didn't because she was a princess and I was holding Moses, so I bowed my head low and said, 'I will, your Royal Highness. I would be honoured,' I said, and I couldn't stop the tears and she must have guessed. But she didn't say anything. She never said anything. Nor did any of her slave-girls. It was a secret we all shared together, us women, the secret of a baby, a Jewish boy baby who was allowed to live. They still didn't say anything even when he didn't need me to feed him any more, and the princess adopted him as her own son and brought him up herself, right under her father's nose. Never said a word. Like the midwives before them.

She's clever my Miriam, a quick thinker. Brave, too.

Being a mother's not easy. All mothers know that. But when you have a Pharaoh on your hands . . . Lots of mothers have pharaohs to cope with, and most pharaohs don't have daughters like that one. Too often the babies get killed. Miriam's the same name as Mary, just its Jewish form. I've heard of another Miriam, in Bethlehem, and her baby boy escaped by the skin of his teeth as well. The other babies in Bethlehem didn't get out in time, apparently.

Soothing God's face

'Moses soothed the face of the Lord his God.' That's a literal translation of the Hebrew of Exodus 32.11. What daring is this! The celebrated King James Bible has, 'Moses besought the Lord his God.' That will not do. It drains the Hebrew of its poetry, its power, its shock. Yet almost all translators follow the KJB's lead. I know of only one published translation, a Jewish one, Everett Fox's The Five Books of Moses, *which gives us the Hebrew straight and refuses to hide it behind some anodyne circumlocution. Yet wonderful though the Hebrew is, its context is deeply unnerving. Exodus 32.1–6 describes the making of the Golden Calf, and in 'soothing his face' Moses is trying to placate a God boiling with rage and threatening to destroy his people.*

In this piece, first published in RE Today *(vol. 29, no. 1, Autumn 2011), I have tried to take the challenge of this passage head on.*

I mean, come on, Moses, what were we supposed to do? We weren't allowed up the mountain. It was God's own holy mountain, and too holy for the likes of us, apparently. So what were we meant to do? Organize a football match? Hadn't been invented. Make pots of jam? You try making jam out of manna. Watch *Countdown* on the telly? No reception. Hang around on street corners? No streets, no corners, but hang around, oh yes. Wait, that's what we had to do. Wait. And then wait some more. You were gone for weeks!

We now know what you were doing all that time. Getting instructions for the tabernacle and all its stuff, and what the priests should wear, and how you should ordain them, and the sacrifices we should offer, and the clouds of incense and all that. Talk about complicated! If George Fox, that Quaker man, had gone up that mountain, he wouldn't have come down with all that flaff. He'd have been back down in half an hour. 'It's all very simple,' he would have said. Come to think of it, good old George would have taken us up there with him.

That's the point, Moses, don't you see? You put yourself between us and God. You got so close to God on the mountain, hidden in the dense mist of its summit, you got so close you could 'soothe his face'. That's what you told us, anyway. We saw the lightning, heard the thunder, and that mysterious trumpet blast. We had the firework show, but we didn't get to see God. You did. We didn't talk with him. You did. As for us soothing his face, forget it. You again, just you.

So we got fed up with this God of yours. We wanted a God down in the camp with us, a God *we* could get close to, a God we could talk to and who would listen, a God we could see, if you can see God at all. Meanwhile you were up there getting instructions for the Temple. Let's face it, Moses, that's what it was about, the grand Temple our grand king would build one day, next to his grand palace, which would mean we would never get close to God, because it would hide him away in a small, cramped room, behind heavy curtains, imprisoned in his Holy of Holies. We wanted a God who was free, a God who was with us, who was fun. That's what the calf was about.

One other thing, Moses, and it's important. This 'soothing God's face' business, what was that about? Why did you have to calm him down? Because he was so wild about the calf we'd made, he was threatening to wipe us off the face of the desert! That's what you said. But that's all wrong and back to front. A God hell-bent on destruction – our children and grandchildren, too, remember – and a human being who has to cajole him into sanity, teach him some compassion! Shouldn't it be *God* who steps in when *we* are threatening to go on the rampage?

It's our violence that needs curbing, our faces full of rage that need to be soothed. Don't make God in our image, Moses. That's idolatry.

Or so you've been telling us.

I do not need your grandeur

The word of the Lord came to Nathan: Go and tell my servant David: Thus says the Lord: Are you the one to build me a house to live in? I have not lived in a house since the day I brought up the people of Israel from Egypt to this day, but I have been moving about in a tent and a tabernacle.

(2 Samuel 7.4–6)

And God says to David,
'Do not make me in your image, your royal highness.
How then could Bedouin shepherds
dare bring me angels' songs and sing them as my
  lullaby?
How could I take my first faltering steps beneath
  the thatch in Nazareth,
or run among the vines,
or dig to find that pearl of great price buried in
  its fields?
How could I sleep in a fishermen's boat,
embrace a madman among the tombs?
How could I talk to a Samaritan woman,
out there at the well in the lonely midday sun,
ask a Zacchaeus to take me to his home?
How could I bend to wash the feet of my friends,
or stoop my head to desert thorns,
stretch my hands and feet against the Romans'
  brutal wood?

'I know what you will do to me in your grand
  cedar house.
You will lock me away and give the key to a high
  priest.
Then he will make me most fearfully holy,
dangerous to approach, deadly to the touch,

and no longer will I be free to say,
"Reach out and put your hand
into the wound upon my side,
extend your finger to my hands,
to the holes that pierce them through."

'And you, the great high king in your fine palace,
will have me next to you,
a god to wear upon the chest,
the *pièce de résistance* of your royal wardrobe.
You will demand prostration of the people,
that all must bow themselves before me
and put their noses in the dust,
when in your heart of hearts
you mean them to lick the dirt from off your
	shoes
and run at the click of your finger.
If I am not careful,
you will ride into Iraq in my name.

'You wish to call me king,
that you may behave like a god,
a god of the old school,
that god of the ancient imaginations
of overweening men.
But my ways are not your ways,
nor ever will be.

'I do not need your grandeur.
I have a grandeur of my own
that reaches far beyond the farthest star.
I bear whole galaxies in the hands you pierced;
the light and dark of space are held in their
	entirety
within the pupils of my eyes;
the universe itself is the smile upon my face.

'I keep my grandeur
in the violet hiding in the shelter of the mountain
    rock,
in the hurtling flight of the falcon,
in the purity of the nightingale's quivering throat
and the cry of the gull against the sea's dark roar,
in the softness of a baby's skin,
in the shuffling of the old man
bearing the tea-tray for his wife
as act of unassuming love,
and in the strong grip of the hand of the dying.

'Do not hide me away,
nor try to pin me down,
fix me as a butterfly inside your case,
for others to admire and think you clever to have
    captured me.
Do not turn the play, the dance of my parables
into the millstones of your doctrine.
I do not want to hang about another's neck,
for their disbelief of what you demand of them
    is true,
be hurled with them into the sea.
I cannot be defined, delineated, described,
however learned you may be.
I will not play your power games,
nor be accessory to your so high authority.
I will not be your prisoner.
I will have my freedom.
You will not domesticate me,
nor make me predictable.
I will come and go as I please,
and if I choose to wash your feet,
then it is not because I am at your beck and call,
but because I love you,

and because your feet are sore
from all your many journeyings.

'A tent is good enough for me,
for I can pack it up and travel with you,
so you can find me where you are,
or else follow in my tracks.
I have a kingdom, David,
very different from your own.
For that a tent will do,
for I can sit outside
and ask you to share with me a glass of tea
and we can tell our stories through the night
and turn it all to day.
And that, my friend, will be all the grandeur we need.'

The house of God

Here we turn first to the wonderful story of Jacob's dream at Beth-El in Genesis 28.10–22, and then to the fiery prophet Amos and his preaching at Beth-El, by then an important shrine in the northern kingdom of Israel, and his famous confrontation with its priest, Amaziah, described in Amos 7.10–17.

The Hebrew word 'beth' means house, and 'el' means God, so 'Beth-El' is 'The House of God'.

Words of God as clear, as clear as a nightingale's
    song,
words that took the dreaming Jacob by surprise,
gave him cause to name the place Beth-El,
The House of God.

The people of the town had no idea
of its sudden, new-found holiness.
They called it Luz,
and didn't change the signs,

when Jacob packed up the promises of God
to take them to Haran.
They slept through his dream,
to find a day like all the rest,
when fields needed sowing,
babies feeding,
and that child who couldn't speak
would need another beating,
to drive the demon out of her.

Jacob had come to their town
on his own and on the run
from a brother out for his crooked blood;
a trickster since he was born,
catching the heel of Esau,
to pull him back to the dark of their mother's
    womb,
lest he be the firstborn son.
When this had failed,
he grew to darker cheating,
drowned a dying father in the filth of shame,
gained the blessing that was his brother's due,
slipped the promises of God in his pocket,
without old Isaac noticing.

This man, of all men,
found the spot where heaven and earth were
    joined;
saw the messengers of God
descending and ascending,
light-laden with the truths of heaven,
heaving up the stairs earth's hopes and agonies;
almost touched his God beside him,
heard a blessing given
when least he could expect it,
not from a dying, duped father,

but from the horse's mouth you might say
(if you wished to be irreverent).

So he did a deal,
promised this surprising God,
that if he would surprise him still
by keeping him fed and watered,
clothed with a safe homecoming at the end of it all,
then he would mark the holiness of the place
by trapping its mystery in carved wood and stone,
song, dance, priest and prophet, pilgrimage and
    festival.

God was as good as his word, of course,
and so Beth-El became more than a name,
a place for touching heaven,
shrine of significance and latent power:
enough to gain the interest of kings
who wished to buy that ancient tale of Jacob's
    dream,
pay good money for his stairway to heaven,
tack their red carpet to its steps.

The place had prophets now,
to curse the king's enemies,
gain for the king the plaudits of heaven
and the blessing of God on lands he had seized.
The place had priests now,
to keep the stairway swept and clean,
darken the air from earth to heaven with smoke of
    sacrifice,
and so make sure the place got up God's nose.

The chief priest was quite a man,
Amaziah.
Able to write was Amaziah,
able to write to the king,

with a turn of a memorable phrase.
Protector of the holy, was he,
protector of the king's high dignity,
keeper of order and propriety.

Those who prophesied at Beth-El under Amaziah
were those authorized to prophesy at Beth-El under
    Amaziah,
prophets who were sons of prophets,
with 'prophet' stamped at the back of their
    passports,
not herdsmen or dressers of sycamore trees –
they were for herding animals and dressing
    sycamores (whatever that was);
that was their place and their function.
To step out of place was to step out of place,
twist the world towards chaos.

So Amos,
self-confessed herdsman and dresser of sycamores,
was not welcome,
barging in at Beth-El,
disrupting the merriment of festival
with his talk of the country's ruin.

Words of God as deep, as deep as a lion's roar
splitting the silence of the night.
Words telling of peasants driven from their land,
sold into slavery,
losing their freedom for a trifle,
the price of a pair of sandals;
no recourse to justice,
no hearing of their case,
courts in the hands of their tormentors;
fleeing to the towns,
to be fleeced again

by those who would sell them the sweepings off
   the floor
and charge them double for the privilege.
Words telling of pilgrims to that Beth-El
lying beside the altars of God,
wrapped warm in the cloaks of the poor,
while those same poor shivered through the
   night's cold.
'Let justice roll down like waters,' Amos roared,
'like the torrent that hurtles down the wadi
when rain spreads its sheet upon the hills!
Let righteousness flow like a spring that never dies,
that even in the heat of summer
turns the ground to life and lush!'

How dare he speak like that!
Who was he to say such things,
neither prophet, nor a prophet's son,
no fine certificate upon his study walls?
Who was *anyone* to say such things,
to spoil the fun of festival,
to blow away the smoke of sacrifice
and see?

So Amaziah sent that pesky little herdsman on
   his way,
and found to his great cost,
when Amos turned,
the sting in his tail.

Eight more centuries passed.

Words of God as clear, as clear as a nightingale's
   song,
words of God as deep, as deep as a lion's roar
splitting the night of Galilee
to reveal the kernel of God's new day;

words of God pointing,
like markers in a wasteland,
to the heart of his kingdom;
words of God that got another prophet into
    trouble
and left him hanging on a cross to die.
No threats this time,
no warning the high priest his wife would be
    a whore,
his sons and daughters killed,
but promising instead to take those hanged
    beside him
to Paradise and the Tree of Life.

Beth-El,
'The House of God',
once Luz,
gained that day a third name.
We call it Golgotha.

Views from the mountains

The two old men sat side by side, their hands folded in their laps, their eyes fixed on moments gone, their memories full of visions.

'I couldn't believe what I'd said to the people,' one of them said. 'I'd been to the very top of the mountain of God, stepped into holiness, come down with my face shining with it. I'd looked into the eyes of God, caught her soft words, one after another. I'd held them, savoured them, placed them carefully in my bag lest any should get lost, taken them down with me and given them to the people, like five loaves and two small fish, so that their lasting hungers might be satisfied. And yet . . . Perhaps the memories of the abuse of Egypt came back to occupy and rule my mind. Perhaps I was brutalized by all that mayhem, by the desolation and dereliction of a land strewn with the bodies of its firstborn. Infanticide on a divine scale. Animals, too. What had *they* done, for God's sake? The price of our salvation, demanded by a saving God! I believed it at the time. I thought it was God's doing, too, when we walked on the water of the Red Sea by stepping on the bodies of drowned Egyptian soldiers.

'But I thought I'd left all that behind me when I found her on Sinai. For I did find the truth there and I saw the goodness of God pass by.

'Yet later, years later, when the sons and daughters of the Sinai people were standing with me near the edge of their Promised Land, I told them that when they entered its towns, they should not let anything that breathed within them remain alive. After seeing God, hearing God, touching, smelling, tasting God, I told them that, stirring them to butchery!

'Then I climbed another mountain and saw the truth a second time. I looked across the valley beneath me and saw the Promised Land for myself. I saw its towns and villages and fields. I saw the men sitting in the sun, conducting their business with one another. I saw the women working in the fields, returning from the wells with their jars of water on their heads. I saw the children out on the hills with the sheep and goats. I saw the younger ones running out from between the houses to greet my people. I saw the babies on their mother's backs, or in their sisters' arms. I saw the old men in front of their houses inviting us to sit with them and rest, until the women could bring some curds and milk and cakes. I saw them. With my own eyes. Too late. I watched in horror as we cut them to pieces. Not one of them left by the end of it. My people had taken my words very seriously.

'Had we come all the way for this? Was this the meaning of a Promised Land? Was this the meaning of *God*? It broke my heart in two. Left it smashed upon the mountain side. I could never forgive myself. What had I done? What had I done, Paul?'

The old men sat side by side and were silent for a long time. The second put his hand upon the other's shoulder. 'I found again the God you touched on Sinai, Moses, my friend,' he said. 'He was marked with the scars of the brutality you saw. "Put your finger here and see my hands," he said to me. "Reach out your hand and put it in my side. Lift up your blinded eyes, and see."

'You saw Jericho. I saw Damascus. Saw the blood of its people on my hands. I too had turned God into a butcher, as you had in Egypt and they did the far side of the Jordan river. Except, of course, he kept his own hands clean and had the likes of me to do his filthy work.

'I was on my way to Damascus to put men and women in chains, to drag them away from their children and haul them back to Jerusalem and their death. I was on my way there for the sake of God's own people, or so I supposed: to repair the wall around them; to keep them safe from the dangers of the world beyond; to hide them from the shamelessness and violence of those outside; to keep them pure, holy, worthy of their God!

'The snows of Hermon were shining above me, but I didn't see them. I had my eyes fixed on the ground, fixed on my next step and on the rhythm of my fear. A fox was lying on the track ahead of me. Vultures were feeding on its body. As I approached, they tried to drag the body away, but I came too close and they lifted, their talons empty, and flew off up the mountain. I stopped for a moment to watch them go. They trailed their sharp shadows over the snows, and suddenly the beauty of their flight stopped my breath. Then it was I heard those words, "Put your finger here and see my hands." I looked down, saw the torn body of the fox and the blood upon my hands, the blood of those men and women and children in Damascus.

'I'd heard many stories about Jesus of Nazareth, how he'd broken down the wall put there to keep us safe; how he'd eaten with people I only knew as sinners; how he'd forgiven a woman caught in adultery, *forgiven* her, washed her feet and served her with bread and wine! He'd gone among the Gentiles and their tombs to find the mad and bring them home! It was outrageous! But not as bad as the trouble he'd caused in the Temple. If the Temple police hadn't stopped him, he would have gone into the sanctuary and torn down the curtain in front of the Holy of Holies, torn it from top to bottom!

'I'd come across his followers in Jerusalem and thought them dangerous enough. In Damascus, so I heard, they were lethal, for their circle included Gentiles. They ate with them, shared the same food, said nothing to their men about circumcision. How could they call themselves Jews and behave like that? They had to be stopped.

'And then, while the vultures soared above the snows of Hermon and the fox lay at my feet, I saw the scars upon my God. It was as if I had put them there. So, like you, I asked myself what I had done.

'I raised my eyes, Moses, my friend, and found a new Promised Land, whose bounds belonged to God's far horizon, where there was room for everyone, and everyone was safe. It was wonderful! It *is* wonderful, my friend.

'Come, let's go on together, as best we may. Lean on one another, that's the trick. I'm beginning to get my bearings in this new Land of God, as well as the measure of her hospitality. It's utterly astonishing, outrageous even. You'll forgive yourself, once you've tasted it, I promise you. I did. Never been the same since.'

5

For special occasions

The yew tree

In the year 2000, as a mark of the millennium, small sapling yew trees were planted up and down the land, which had been grown from cuttings taken from particularly ancient trees. Yews can live to a very great age, and the cuttings came from plants that were thought to be as much as two thousand years old. They thus presented a direct, living link with the time when Jesus was born. The following piece is an edited version of one first written for the planting of one of these saplings in a churchyard in the centre of Chester.

In Bethlehem, two thousand years ago, a baby's cry split the dark of a long, unbending winter's night. The angels took up their trumpets, trombones and tubas, and blew off the roof of heaven. Shepherds brought the pungent smells of fields and sheep and goats to a manger and found themselves, to their astonishment, looking straight into the face of God. They gave him presents of a fleece to keep him warm, a pipe to play when he grew up, and a bunch of wild winter flowers. To Mary and Joseph they presented a goat's cheese, a skin of wine and, with unwitting prophecy, a slaughtered lamb.

In the north-west of England (as now we call it), that very night, that self-same night of Bethlehem, some shepherds gathered upon their local holy ground, to play their pipes and dance, and offer up to God their gifts of cheese and wool. The place was marked by an ancient tree, a yew. Mistle thrushes nested in its branches, and many birds found safe roosting in the darkness of its foliage. Spiders festooned it with their webs, great tits and greenfinches ate its seed, while winter redwings and fieldfares came to feast on the rich flesh of its berries. Which had come first, the tree, or the holiness of the place? No one knew and no one cared. This they knew: the tree and the ground on which it stood were holy. That was enough.

The yew's green never faded. It could withstand the drought and heat of the driest, hottest summers, the ice and snow of the coldest winters. Storms that toppled other trees left it untouched. It seemed immortal, veined with mystery. The shepherds were often glad of its shade, or its shelter against the gale or the rain, but on the night that Christ was born they sought it for its holiness. A wind blew through its branches and made a strange sound, like the distant crying of a child. They stopped their dance and put down their pipes to listen.

The yew tree is still there. Today, when you stand at its foot and look up into its branches, you see not so much a tree as a small wood. The centre of the tree is all but gone, left as a blackened shell, so thin that it is peppered with peepholes. Strange beasts can be found there, shaped by the weather over the centuries, a camel's head, a sheep's skull. Yet around this centre three fluted trunks still mark out its life. Their flaked bark is grey and fawn, silver, russet and fox bright. In places it seems the old tree has forgotten to shave that day, that week, for leaves sprout from the surface of the trunks, like the stubble of a green beard. No one would call it a tidy tree. Branches spread in all directions, and its crown is not a single, elegant curve, but allows many an inlet for the sky. Mistle thrushes still nest in its branches and rear their young to sound like clockwork toys. Great tits and greenfinches still eat its seed, redwings and fieldfares still take its berries against the winter's cold, wrens and goldcrests still find safety in its dark, and spiders still adorn it with their silk.

Yet one thing has changed. Beside the tree a Christian church now stands. Inside the church, and in processions round its bounds, branches of this ancient yew were once used on Palm Sundays to usher Jesus into his Jerusalem, and as signs at funerals of ongoing life and resurrection. Those days are gone. The tree is left untouched now. Its branches are not taken to church any more. Yet still it lends the church a special mystery, offers it its great longevity. After all, it has stood on the spot for so long, growing tall before the church was built, first piercing the surface of the ground before there were any churches of any kind in any place. Slowly year by year, century by century, it has filled its girth, until eventually, as a holy tree should when standing beside a Christian church, it has split into a trinity.

The tree goes down deeper than we know. It belongs to the earth from which it grows, and will stay there rooted to the spot for ever, or so it seems. It spreads its wonderful untidiness to the ragged sky, its weight more than even the most legendary of giants could lift.

Yet see here! This small beginning of a yew tree is its child! This cutting, which has its own roots now, its very own attachments to the earth, this tiny tree, in which one day mistle thrushes will nest and spiders hang their webs, this small, delicate plant, this mark of God's imagination, which you can hold quite easily in your hand, this is two thousand years old! It comes from a stream of life which flows without ceasing past innumerable wars, past the plays of Shakespeare, past the great cathedrals of our land, past 1066 and all that, past Viking raids, past monks sailing Christ across the sea, past the burning of a temple in Jerusalem, past a cross on Calvary, past an unexpected heaven let loose in Galilee, all the way to a long, unbending winter's night in Bethlehem.

A true Christmas tree, if ever there was one!

This place has fallen silent

A meditation composed for an evening service in the Lady Chapel of Chester Cathedral. It draws upon many details of the building, though there is one significant omission. On the east wall of that chapel now hang two wonderful Russian icons, and a third is displayed on a stand just outside it, all three of them painted in the Russian Orthodox parish of Kondopoga in Karelia, with which the Cathedral is linked. This meditation dates from a time before those icons arrived.

This place has fallen silent.
Even the candles lit by those
who came to pray,
to bear in fragile flame
their needs or longings,
their guilt or fear,
their pleas to God for loved ones,
missing, sick, departed,
even those are burned out now,
while Mary and her small child,
taking his first steps
and looking up to her for reassurance,
these two light figures, shaped in thin copper
    sheets,
are left to carry the prayers
into the heart of God.
The place is still now.

The crowds of visitors are gone,
and the notes of the organ
marking the end of Evensong
have long since died in this sacred air.
The choristers have had their tea by now,
finished their homework,
the younger ones already fast asleep in bed.

In past years ravens would have been building
    their nest,
high on the tower,
knitting together twigs snapped from the trees
    below,
bridging the gap between gargoyle and ledge,
lining the circle of the nest bowl
with sheep's wool brought from the fields,
ringing it round with yellow strands of willow
carried from the tree in the Bishop's garden –
a small masterpiece of engineering,
a safe place for eggs to be laid
and for young to grow to fledging.
But the ravens are not here any more,
and even if they were,
they would have ended their day's work by now,
turned to keeping silent vigil on the parapet.

Sometimes the wail of sirens
penetrates the thick stone of the walls,
as ambulance, police car, or fire engine
races through the city streets
to remind us that not all is well
and bids us pray for those in sudden need.
But in between
this place keeps its silence.

It is more than an absence of noise.
There is a deeper silence to be found here,
one that remains on the busiest of days,
even when hundreds of children fill the air
with their excited chatter or their song,
a quiet that is the very silence of God.
God treads softly here,
and if we keep still for a moment,
we will hear.

Others keep us company.
Behind us, high on the painted roof of the Quire,
the angels are gathered with their instruments,
a veritable orchestra, straight from heaven,
while closer to our backs
the tiny figure of St Werburgh
stands in her shrine,
to mark the spot
where so many centuries of pilgrims came to
    pray,
amidst the singing of the monks.
Above our heads,
carved in intricate bosses
strung down the middle of the vault,
are a Trinity,
God the Father,
bearing his Son in his arms,
still hanging on his cross,
with the dove of the Holy Spirit
alighted on the cross's arm;
a Mary and her child, also,
her double-curving body
protected by angels
sending incense up to heaven
from their swinging thuribles;
and then, close to the shrine of the saint,
murder,
the slaughter of St Thomas Becket –
four soldiers plunging in their swords,
while he stands at the altar
and holds aloft the consecrated host,
the sign of the presence of God,
at the very heart of the Eucharist.
It is a shocking image
to find in this quiet, holy space.

Yet there is one more shocking still,
that one of the Son of God crucified;
God himself flogged,
hammered to twisted wood,
the most degrading death the Romans knew,
kept for the lowest of the low
and those of no account who dared defy their
   power.
Crucified naked,
on a post six or seven feet tall,
thorns biting into his head,
fighting for breath:
that was where in truth we left our God.
The angels covered their faces from the sight,
the swirling galaxies stopped,
and the burning sun went out
and plunged us into dark.
The earth shivered, shook in the cold
of that fearful death.
It was as if God had died.
It was as simple, as shattering as that.

Yet see, yet see,
there is another cross here,
standing in the middle of the altar table,
its silver turned side on,
so you can hardly see it.
It is empty!
Have they taken him away for burial?
It is an urgent question,
laden with our fear,
for we know the Romans
often left the bodies
hanging on the crosses they had made,
so the wild animals and the birds

could feast themselves
and finish the careful degradation.

His friends did take him down,
gave him burial in a rich man's tomb,
and the women came to honour him,
anoint his body
and make him smell sweet to high heaven.
Yet that is not why the cross here
no longer bears his body.
The spices and perfumes the women brought
were not needed.
They did not find his corpse.
They found nothing in the tomb,
except angels.
They came for death,
and stumbled into life eternal.

Yet they did not recognize where they were,
until they got beyond the angels
and met their friend again,
and knew him then
for the first time
as their Lord and their God.

The marks of nails and spear were still upon him.
He met them as a wounded God.
They had never known or dreamed of such a thing.
But then no one had.

This is the God we can find again,
find within touching distance,
as Mary of Magdala and Thomas did,
and when we do,
we will know ourselves loved,
embraced,
held tight against the world's cruelties,

and we will be given the spirit, the energy
to help God build his kingdom here on earth.

How must we respond?

*This was composed for a service in Chester Cathedral on the Sunday
after the terrorist bombings in London, on 7 July 2005, when there
were three explosions on the underground and a bus was blown
apart. Many people died, and many more were injured.*

How must we respond,
we to whom the man from Nazareth
has shown the heart of God?
How must we respond,
when dark warnings come to terrible fruition,
when trains are buckled in black tunnels by
    fearful blast,
and a bus's upper seats are shown to the morning
    sun;
when people do not arrive at work
and desks are empty,
when morning farewells turn out to have been
    too casual,
a quick peck on the cheek and 'See you, love'
    not enough;
when people in uniforms run towards danger,
and priests sit to hold the hands of bleeding
    men who cannot speak;
when too many sirens rush their sounds along
    the streets,
and there is too much blood,
too much sudden death,
too much fighting for life,
too much for too many
who will never be the same again?

How must we respond?
Not by talking talk of war,
be it war on terror, on extremists, on al-Qaida.
See what war on terror has produced so far,
if not more fear, more hate, more terror still.

How must we respond,
we to whom the man from Nazareth
has shown the heart of God?
Not by dehumanizing those who make such bombs
and place them with their careful calculation,
or carry them on their backs, or strapped to their
    chests,
who know you don't need hordes of Herod's
    soldiers
to make a massacre of innocents
and bring more tears to Rachel's eyes.
Their truth is too uncomfortable,
yet must be faced.
For they who plot and split and rip,
they too belong to our humanity,
their rage too close for comfort,
their blindness touching on our dark.
Their hatred,
their unblinking desire to hit back,
their all-consuming passion for destruction –
these are not entirely strangers to us.
And they too are children of God,
called into his circle,
their places waiting empty,
the bowl of water ready for God
to wash their bloodied feet,
their shrugging shoulders needing his embrace
as much as ours.
God has numbered the hairs on their heads, also,

has their names too inscribed on the palms of his hands.
They are not monsters,
though they have done such monstrous things;
terrorism is not all they do,
nor the sum of their humanity.
We must pray for them
as well as for their victims,
pray that they emerge from their stinking dark
and see the light in those they count their enemy,
and the kindness in the eyes of God,
the Most Gracious, the Most Merciful,
pray that they may come to feel his touch
and know the ways that make for peace.
Let us not share their hate
and cry for their destruction.
Let us pray instead for their turning to the arms of God,
though now they crush the crown of thorns down
    on his scalp again
with such sincere relish.

Let us not hate,
but learn the ways of peace
from those who went racing to the horrors,
who went down into tunnels and smoking twisted
    trains,
who counted the dead,
who held the wounded,
who spoke gently to the frightened,
who put rehearsed plans into swift operation,
who did their jobs without flinching,
who came down from scaffolding to give their blood,
who waited in the hospitals for the ambulances to
    arrive,
got the operating theatres ready,
went about their work with calm efficiency,

who opened churches' doors,
put the kettle on,
made the loos available,
gave some quiet to exhausted men
who had seen things none of us should see.

Nor let us race to blame,
to say that they whose job it is to know,
they should have known,
they should have seen,
they should have nipped it in the bud,
thus hiding from ourselves
our ignorance and fallibility,
concealing the shame of our mistakes.

Let us learn again the ways of God,
the paths that lead unerringly to peace,
set loose our generosity,
make habits of our courtesies,
be kinder to one another.
Let us follow the man from Galilee,
let him take us through the narrow gate,
to go the extra mile,
to turn the other cheek,
to repay evil with good,
to repay evil with good.

That is a hard road,
but all others lead to perdition.

Words dance in sacred space

This was first composed for a wedding held in the Lady Chapel of Chester Cathedral. Helping prepare the couple, Ann and Stewart, for that great day and for their married life beyond was a delight. They told me straightaway that they wanted to keep their plans for the wedding as simple as possible, so they could concentrate on the vows they would be making. They were as good as their word.

The readings they chose for the service were from the Song of Songs 2.10–13; 8.6–7, and from the Sermon on the Mount, Matthew 5.1–10. At that time Harold Gosney's wonderful statue of Mary teaching the toddler Jesus to walk, since moved to the north choir aisle, was placed in the Chapel's sanctuary, facing the shrine of St Werburgh at the other end.

The piece is reproduced here with Ann's and Stewart's permission.

Words dance in sacred space
and fill the air between,
words of ancient passion:
Arise my love, my fair one
and come away . . .
an invitation to elope that is not needed here,
yet words that shine with tenderness,
such triumphant delight and beauty
that are quite in place;
words that with the image of a seal
catch all the intimacy of love,
its preciousness and rare commitment,
the longing it last for ever,
the belief it can:
Set me as a seal upon your heart . . .
stamp me on your heart,
upon your limbs.
Sear my emblem deep into your skin . . .
the love that can outlive death,
and still burn,
like the flames of a Burning Bush,
even when the waters surge to drown them;
timeless words of a Jewish peasant poet,
Son of God, no less,
that fall like manna

upon the desert floor
of our aggressive world,
talk of
the meek inheriting the earth,
of mercy
and of making peace.

Words dance in sacred space
and fill the air between.

Already we have heard from you, Ann and Stewart,
words of loving,
comforting,
honouring,
protecting,
of forsaking all others;
already your 'I will', 'I will'
have made commitment loud
and called forth cries of support
and outpouring of divine blessing.
And soon,
in this most unfussy of weddings,
where all that is inessential has been left aside,
and all that is essential put in the centre,
vows will be made and made,
vows for each and every time such as this,
vows for *this* time,
this place,
these two,
these two of you,
vows to bind,
to hold,
to set you free,
that you may play and grow and flourish
within their bright space;
vows designed to draw the very best,

vows to speak the things of God.
And more, more words will soon be spoken
over small circles of gold
held on extended hands:
All that I am I give to you,
all that I have I share with you . . .
these words too
will dance in sacred space and fill the air,
fill the air between an ancient battered shrine,
where once they came to touch the hem of heaven,
and a young, fragile, pierced woman
teaching the Son of God to walk;
fill the air between the murder of an archbishop
and a God bearing the body of his crucified Son
(these cruel things set in the roof above our heads
lest we become too sentimental,
or forget the pain of God
and the quiet power of love),
these will fill the air with giving,
giving all,
giving unreservedly.

You will not forget this day,
Stewart and Ann,
nor this holy place,
nor the words that fill its waiting air.
All that is here speaks of the generosity of love,
to remind you, as the years go by,
to challenge and inspire you,
to delight you,
to put even death in its place.

You will have spoken the truth here,
here in this little holy space,
where truth is held so dear.
May the God of blessings bless you.

Remembering Tess

Tessa Massey, known to all as Tess, was a remarkable woman, at the centre of a remarkable family. My wife was at university with her younger daughter Sally, and through their friendship we got to know Tess and her husband, Austin, and their elder daughter whom everyone called Pooh, and grew very fond of them all. When Tess eventually died in her old age, a few years after her beloved Austin, the family asked me to take her funeral and give an address. It was an enormous privilege. It always is, of course. When I sat down to compose the address I found myself turning to the poetic form: it better allowed me to say what I wanted to say and express something of what I felt.

The family have kindly given their permission to include the piece here.

'A free spirit.'
That's what everyone says,
and everyone is right.
She taught us how to be free, did Tess,
showed us the nature of freedom,
not the I-did-it-my-way-and-to-hell-with
   anyone-else
kind of thing,
which is no freedom at all,
but the wide-open-space of the freedom of love –

her enduring love for Austin,
the husband she held for so long,
yet died a few years too soon;
for Pooh and Sally, the children of their love;
for all her grandchildren,
Anna and Helen and Katie and Rosie and Robert;
for her great-grandchildren, Austin (another Austin!)
   and Bonnie;
for old friends made for life,

Kitt Hope among them, and Daphne Lack;
for her own parents who lived so very long,
her mother longer than she did herself.

It was a warm, generous, gracious, most welcoming
     love,
persistent, persisting,
forgiving, down-to-earth,
understanding and hugely compassionate,
sacrificial,
months at a time staying with her parents
in their great old age, looking after them,
then fourteen years her mother living with them in
     their home,
fourteen years of care till one day, at 104,
at last her mother died.
A homely, home-making love –
serving tea in the garden,
properly,
with teapot, hot water jug, and cake;
sending off her daughters to parties in dresses she
     had made,
but not quite finished,
sewing them in and cutting them out,
buttons and buttonholes still to come;
stitching a quilt made of all her off-cuts;
teaching her grandchildren to sew and to cook,
and set the table,
properly;
giving them ditties to help with their spelling,
'E G Y Perteee, Egypt';
making up stories for them about a Henry Heath,
who later they discovered, to their great surprise,
had lived outside her storytelling;
playing the piano,

even into the darkness of her Alzheimer's
(for that, alas, became hers, too).

And her beauty –
'She gets more beautiful every time I see her':
not many have that said about them when they are
   well past 70 years;
her elegance,
cast to the winds in her beloved garden,
when she gave place to the greater beauty of flowers,
and dressed appropriately,
a real scruff,
so far from the Tess Massey at weddings,
in hats to die for,
Pooh and Sally, too,
all hats she'd made herself,
with a carefully trained, precise needle,
and a natural, bright creativity.

In the darkness of her rapid fall into Alzheimer's,
once Austin had so suddenly
driven into a wall and died,
when Sally read her poetry
to bring some calm to her inner chaos,
and Pooh and David,
being close at hand,
did day after day what she had once done for her
   own mother,
and stretched out to her their own persisting,
   sacrificial love,
did she ever remember the time
when she and Austin had sold strawberries
at the top of Codmore Hill
to people climbing out of coaches –
a punnet and a bunch of sweet peas for half
   a crown?

In the moments of her lucidity,
did she swing her mind back
to her convent school in Belgium,
and the meals held in holy silence,
till the puddings came
and a nun clapped to say that speaking was allowed
(what agonies those silences must have held for
     Tess!)?
Did she remember writing home to say,
'If I'm good can I come home?'?

If I'm good can I come home?
Oh yes, oh yes, you can,
Tess Massey,
for there is one
whose love is warmer still than yours,
more generous, more gracious,
more welcoming still,
more persistent and persisting,
more forgiving and compassionate,
sacrificial to the point of crucifixion,
who runs up the road to meet you,
bringing Austin with him,
to hold you tight in embrace
held for an eternity,
and remake you
as first he made you,
the twinkle in his eye.

And he will want you, Tess,
to create for him a new hat,
as fine as fine as ever you conceived.
For it is time he took off the crown of thorns
we have plaited for him;
time we gave him something to dress up in
for the feasting of heaven.

And you can lead him in, Tess,
(for God is like that,
and never stands on any dignity),
and he can show his new hat to the angels,
and if we stop and listen carefully,
then we will hear their cheers go up,
and in our tears we will,
with Tess and Austin Massey,
laugh.

The ocean of God's love

I composed this piece during a five-day retreat I was leading for the Sisters of the Order of the Holy Paraclete at St Hilda's Priory in Whitby, on the North Yorkshire coast. I delivered it at the end of my final address. I found them a profoundly inspiring community – and not so elderly as my mischievous mention of Zimmer frames might suggest!

In one line I introduce the Hebrew phrase ruah 'elohim, *which means the spirit or wind of God. It first occurs in the Bible in Genesis 1.2, where the* ruah *is described as quivering upon the face of the waters at the creation of the world.* Ruah *is a noun of feminine gender, as I make plain.*

Too often, too persistent
the fog settles dense about our minds
and turns our souls to grey;
or else we cannot see through steam and smoke of
    ceaseless activity;
our ears, plugged with incessant beat,
hear nothing out of ordinary.

And yet, at times beyond price
the Son burns off the mist,
we cease our busyness and look;
we free our ears to hear the distant roar;

we top the ridge
and find an Ocean there
of which we'd never dreamed,
or if we had,
we knew not its reality.

It flashes with the lights of heaven,
pointing not the greyness of our familiar sea,
but turquoise, emerald, sapphire, silver, lapis
    lazuli, amber into gold.

Once seen
it can never be forgot,
and we can do no other than scramble down
    the slipping scree,
sliding on our Zimmer frames
to take the narrow path towards the shore.

Once there,
what will we do?
Look on amazed?
But that is not enough.
Be overcome with love?
If that is all,
call it but infatuation,
for then we are trenched in sentiment.
Might we strip ourselves,
daringly,
for a paddle,
so we can splash and kick and whoop
and play the child again?
Might we fold up our fears, our comfort
    blankets,
and leave them on the sand
beside our proud, fragile castles,
step in,

anxiously,
fearing the cold,
then strangely warmed,
wade out more boldly,
till curling waves collapse about our waists,
we lift our feet from certainty,
and swim?
We might.
Dare we, dare we swim out of our depth,
or even this,
over God's horizon,
out of range of all we know, are comforted by?
Or else search out a boat,
fill its sails with the Spirit-Wind of God,
that skittish *ruah 'elohim*,
let her take us where she wills,
beyond all bound and shore?

We might, we might!
We cannot drown,
for these are the Waters of Life.
There is no risk of bursting lungs,
for God bears all the pressures of the deep.
There is no dark,
for all is Light,
no Son to lose as we sink down.

Gannets and squealing terns will tilt and dive,
to spear the surface full of holes,
not for fish,
but for the sheer heaven of it
(for these are the seas of God's making,
of God's very being,
and the fish are God's fish also);
dolphins will turn somersaults,
whales will give us rides,

shearwaters teach us how to fly in the teeth of
  the gale.
These will be God's angels,
our constant and our playful companions.

Our journey will never be done.
The swell and sway of this Ocean
are all eternity,
the glittering infinity of Love.